T0331237

YOUR LEGACY
IS NOW

YOUR LEGACY IS NOW

Life Is Not a Search for Meaning
from Others—It's the Creation
of Meaning for Yourself

ALAN WEISS

Routledge
Taylor & Francis Group

First published 2021
by Routledge
600 Broken Sound Parkway #300, Boca Raton FL, 33487

and by Routledge
2 Park Square, Milton Park, Abingdon, Oxon, OX14 4RN
Routledge is an imprint of the Taylor & Francis Group, an informa business

© 2021 Taylor & Francis

The right of Alan Weiss to be identified as author of this work has been asserted by him in accordance with sections 77 and 78 of the Copyright, Designs and Patents Act 1988.

All rights reserved. No part of this book may be reprinted or reproduced or utilised in any form or by any electronic, mechanical, or other means, now known or hereafter invented, including photocopying and recording, or in any information storage or retrieval system, without permission in writing from the publishers.

Trademark notice: Product or corporate names may be trademarks or registered trademarks, and are used only for identification and explanation without intent to infringe.

ISBN: 9780367723194 (hbk)
ISBN: 9781003154372 (ebk)

Typeset in Garamond
by Deanta Global Publishing Services, Chennai, India

Contents

We don't seem to know what we mean by "meaning," let alone "legacy." We focus on what we do, not who we are. We are easy "prey" for normative pressures to mold us or even distort us. We need to escape the "ruts" that often unseen others create for us. To do so, we need to examine our beliefs and values as well as our vision for ourselves. Yet most people have trouble answering the question, "Who do you want to be next year?"

There are origins of competitiveness that are no longer valid but which continue to influence us. What difference does it make standing up to retrieve baggage in a plane parked at the gate after landing? We compete about inconsequential things, often unaware of our own actions. Yet there are times when appropriate competition is a great reconciler and consensus builder. But what are the boundaries? Our legacy is too often tied to others' (often dysfunctional) behaviors.

Size is often a disadvantage (try to parallel park an SUV), and strength today is not totally reliant on human muscle. The "super fit" and the careful dieters are often those who drop from heart attacks in the streets. Our advertising and corporate promotion are often unconsciously directed to the wrong appeal. Our legacy shouldn't be "nth" or "est." Why do we praise miniaturization and agility in some aspects (microchips, sports cars) but think we need a 20-room mansion to be comfortable or food hanging off our plates to enjoy a good meal?

Legacy is amazingly pragmatic and "in the trenches." Street smarts aren't taught, they're learned, but not all over, and they provide proportion. David would win every time, and Voltaire observed that "God is on the side of the heaviest battalions." The amount and size of your prayers don't make you more likely to reach heaven. Luther simply wanted a hearing but the Pope wanted to make an example of him and he inadvertently changed the world. Once you're an "underdog" in people's perceptions, you're no longer an underdog in reality.

Bigger, faster, better: they carefully measure with chains for a first down in football after the ball is arbitrarily placed where an official's foot marks the forward progress. Does a hundredth-second victory in a swim or footrace really indicate superiority? Just whose legacy are we talking about? The mediocre thrive on arbitrary assessments of merit and we succumb to it, from Nathan's Hot Dog Eating Contest to America's Got Talent (apparently, not all the time).

Counterintuitively, perhaps, legacy is about humility. As humans, we need to connect and interact. This requires vulnerability and reciprocity. It also requires honesty. We talk about "sportsmanship" and "how you play the game" amidst doping scandals and cheating. Even the lofty Olympics plays the national anthem only of the winner, who stands on a podium above others, and maintains a medal count during the games. Our competition and the caste system it creates are the antithesis of connecting and communicating.

We compete for mates. Why is there such a disproportionate number of beautiful women on the arms of professional male athletes? Why is the divorce rate so high among celebrities? Why does the Wall Street Journal have a weekly section on "Mansions"? The competition at the top of society fosters similar behavior down the ladder and is accepted as normal, with "lifestyle" replacing intimacy, the gross revenues of a performance replacing artistic merit, and the manifestation of luxury overwhelming intimacy. (There is also always a bigger house.)

If we weren't so competitive we wouldn't cheat so much, and we wouldn't find so many ingenious ways to cheat. The Nazis tried to rig the 1936 Olympics, Rosie Ruiz took the subway to try to win the New York Marathon, and drug testing is now a standard accompaniment of all major sports. We cheat because "winning" has become mindlessly addictive, even in cutting a line to board a plane or sneaking into the members-only airline club. A Harvard rowing coach who was asked about his team finishing last in the Olympics commented, "Since when is there anything to be ashamed about by being eighth best in the world?"

We become paranoid about "being caught from behind," and adhere to mindless admonitions about discipline and focus lest we're surprised by someone highly unlikely passing us by. In law firms it's "up or out," in universities "publish or perish," on New Hampshire license plates, "live free or die." Isn't there some comfortable middle ground here? Legacy is daily, you don't have to worry about someone beating you to the finish line or even beating you to the punch.

The grass may be greener, but so the hell what? How green can green be? That's in the eye of the beholder. Happiness has to be on our own terms, not from some celebrity, or glossy magazine, or braggart neighbor. You have to be comfortable sailing through life in the manner that pleases you. It's not about the size of the craft, because there is always going to be a bigger boat. I'll show you mine if you show me yours.

About the Author

Alan Weiss is one of those rare people who can say he is a consultant, speaker, and author and mean it. His consulting firm, Summit Consulting Group, Inc., has attracted clients such as Merck, Hewlett-Packard, GE, Mercedes-Benz, State Street Corporation, Times Mirror Group, the Federal Reserve, The New York Times Corporation, Toyota, and over 200 other leading organizations. He has served on the board of directors of the Trinity Repertory Company, a Tony-Award-winning New England regional theater, as President of the Board of Festival Ballet Providence, and chaired the Newport International Film Festival.

His speaking typically includes 20 keynotes a year at major conferences, and he has been a visiting faculty member at Case Western Reserve University, Boston College, Tufts, St. John's, the University of Illinois, the Institute of Management Studies, UC Berkeley, and the University of Georgia Graduate School of Business. He has held an appointment as adjunct professor in the Graduate School of Business at the University of Rhode Island where he taught courses on advanced management and consulting skills. He once held the record for selling out the highest priced workshop (on entrepreneurialism) in the then-21-year history of New York City's Learning Annex. His PhD is in psychology. He has served on the Board of Governors of Harvard Medical School Center for Mental Health and the Media.

He is an inductee into the Professional Speaking Hall of Fame® and the concurrent recipient of the National Speakers Association Council of Peers

Award of Excellence, representing the top 1% of professional speakers in the world. He has been named a Fellow of the Institute of Management Consultants, one of only two people in history holding both those designations.

His prolific publishing includes over 500 articles and 60+ books, including his best-seller, *Million Dollar Consulting* (from McGraw-Hill). His books have been on the curricula at Villanova, Temple University, Stanford University, and the Wharton School of Business, and have been translated into 16 languages.

He is interviewed and quoted frequently in the media. His career has taken him to 63 countries and 49 states. (He is afraid to go to North Dakota.) *Success Magazine* cited him in an editorial devoted to his work as "a worldwide expert in executive education." The *New York Post* called him "one of the most highly regarded independent consultants in America." He is the winner of the prestigious Axiem Award for Excellence in Audio Presentation.

He is the recipient of the Lifetime Achievement Award of the American Press Institute, the first-ever for a non-journalist, and one of only seven awarded in the 65-year history of the association.

He has coached former Miss Rhode Island/Miss America candidates in interviewing skills. He once appeared on the popular American TV game show *Jeopardy!*, where he lost badly in the first round to a dancing waiter from Iowa.

Alan has been married to the lovely Maria for 52 years, and they have two children and twin granddaughters. They reside in East Greenwich, RI, with their dogs, Coco and Bentley, a white German Shepherd.

Other Works by Alan Weiss

Million Dollar Referrals
Million Dollar Speaking (also in Chinese, Portuguese)
Million Dollar Web Presence
Money Talks (also in Chinese)
Organizational Consulting
Our Emperors Have No Clothes
Process Consulting
The Business Wealth Builders (with Phil Symchych)
The Consulting Bible (also in Portuguese)
The DNA of Leadership (with Myron Beard)
The Global Consultant
The Great Big Book of Process Visuals
The Innovation Formula (with Mike Robert) (also in German, Italian)
The Language of Success (with Kim Wilkerson)
The Resilience Advantage (with Richard Citrin)
The Son of the Great Big Book of Process Visuals
The Talent Advantage (with Nancy MacKay)
The Ultimate Consultant
The Unofficial Guide to Power Management
The Power of Strategic Commitment (with Josh Leibner and Gershon Mader)
Threescore and More
Thrive!
Value Based Fees
Who's Got Your Back?

Introduction

The Wright brothers first achieved powered flight at Kitty Hawk in 1903 for about 12 seconds and covered 120 feet. Sixty-six years later we landed a man on the moon, traveling 480,000 miles over 8 days. That's well within one person's lifetime.

A legacy is not what's written in an obituary, nor spoken over a casket, nor written about people years after their death. Legacy is what we create *every day*, not some tally at the end of our lives. I believe that legacy is the result of creating meaning continually—not searching for it in distant places or in eccentric experiences.

As you can see in Figure X.1, you need a high ability to act coupled with high self-awareness to create meaning and legacy. Otherwise, you're helpless to act or oblivious to the need to act or, worst of all, *a bystander to your own life, a mere observer.*

Meaning is about the impact and significance of our lives. We don't search for it in others, though we may create it through our associations with others. This is a daily possibility. We don't need to mark our calendars with "10:30, create some meaning as a contribution to my legacy." But we do need to stop moving through our lives and the world in an automated, insensitive, and unappreciative manner.

It's not merely about "smelling roses," but more about understanding why people enjoy smelling roses, and why we take them for granted when they're not in a vase directly under our noses.

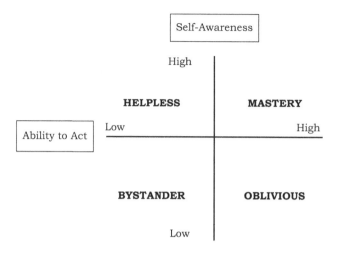

Figure X.1 *Self-awareness and the ability to act.*

Life is short, even for the longest-lived of us. It's a shame to believe that people will appreciate and comment on our contributions only when we've died! It's vital that we appreciate whatever and whomever we can while we're able to do so, and that includes appreciating our own contributions.

My intent is that you engage in mastery in terms of your self-awareness of these factors and your ability to act. As you can see in the chart, too many of us are merely bystanders to our own lives.

My goal in writing *Legacy* is that you will have the skills, behaviors, and motivation to create meaning in your life as a natural aspect of your existence. If you can do that, you'll create your legacy, just as your reading this book is helping to add to mine.

Alan Weiss
East Greenwich, RI
January 2021

CHAPTER 1

Don't Search for Meaning, Create Meaning

We are simultaneously arrogant and humble, like an athlete who trains hard but is embarrassed by winning. We think we know far more than we do because we focus on knowns and not unknowns—confirmation bias on steroids. Yet most of us believe it's inappropriate to blow our own horns or proclaim our own contributions.

But if you don't blow your own horn, there is no music.

Fairy Tales

Harvard University chair of department and psychology rock star Dan Gilbert has been studying happiness for a long time. One of his research findings showed that people who claimed they attended church regularly were happier than those who responded that they did not. *However, this did not correlate with belief in God, where there was no statistical difference in happiness with non-believers.* Dan's conclusion is that church attendance embraces people in a community and that such inclusion creates more happiness than isolation.

In fact, it's become fashionable today to look down our sophisticated noses at those who are people of faith, never mind their IQs, successes or positions of responsibility. The late essayist Christopher Hitchens and the ubiquitous evolutionary biologist Richard Dawkins have been anti-religious (not "merely" atheistic) with a religious fervor rarely attained by the faithful.

Their condescension for believers has been equaled only by Hillary Clinton's blanket slandering of the people who didn't support her as "deplorables."

Christianity, of course, is about tolerance and forgiveness, but it's a dark horse in this race. The Biblical creation story is mocked as a fairy tale to be accepted only by the mouth breathers and knuckle-scrapers (in other words, "deplorables").

There is a creation fairy tale, to be sure, in fact more than one. And the one that strikes me as the most ludicrous is that first there was nothing, then there was something, then that something blew apart, and over millennia solar systems were created and on our planet life was somehow born from non-living materials to eventually evolve into huge predatory monsters only halted by a huge piece of space junk, and then rerouted into sentience, the eyeball, opposable thumbs, and mini-marts.

Whew!

Let me take a breath. That's better than *Game of Thrones* and *Harry Potter* combined.

Thus, our hubris. We try to organize the mysterious universe around us with technology and science, sometimes fitting things like quarks and prions and gluons together into a cosmic jigsaw puzzle, equivalent to our cutting pieces off regular jigsaw puzzle pieces of dogs playing cards to make them fit better. We actually think we understand the universe when virtually no one can understand anything Stephen Hawking ever wrote.

In fact, if you simply point at the sky, no one can tell you where you would end up in a million years. We don't know what's out there. Einstein proved there were laws governing the clockwork as far as it went, but even he raised the question, "But who or what created the laws?"

Therefore, as much as we may find it stylish to condemn the beliefs embedded in religions, we are very willing to accept the beliefs of science which haven't been proved nor duplicated, which is what science tradition-ally prides itself about in a kind of pious, monastic impeccability.

There's the arrogance. The belief that we actually know our origins, know our present condition, even know our destiny which, outside of religious belief, is apparently merely food for microbes. Yet if I ask anyone—and I have asked thousands in the last 20 years—"Do you believe there is life in the universe other than us?" I get only three answers:

Yes.
No.
I don't know.

What would you answer?

The point is that *any of those answers is mind-blowing*. If we're sharing the universe with as yet unknown creatures, will we find them or will they find us? Will they be primitive or advanced? Will they barter with us or use us as paper clips?

If there is no other life, then what the hell are we doing here alone in a cosmos the dimensions of which we can't even comprehend? Is this someone's bad joke? Or are we the billion-to-one shot that bankrupts Vegas?

Finally, if we just don't know, well, we're not all that certain or clever, are we? What will it take to convince us one way or the other? A close encounter of the third kind?

I think you can see the segue to humility. We *are* lost in space, and a great deal of our confidence quickly evaporates when we view the picture using a different frame. We begin to question why "bad things happen to good people," we don't want to be seen as "imposers" in the eyes of others, we tell each other that humility is a key to success.

Yet what is "humility"? It certainly isn't the demeaning of one's own talents and achievements. I think of it as a respect for others as equals without a diminishment of one's own identity. No one has ever screamed for a humble heart surgeon, or trial lawyer, or consultant. If your chest is going to be opened by strangers in a sterile room, you want a surgeon who thinks they're a few steps ahead of God. You'd want a divorce attorney who drools aggression and total command.

Humility ain't what it's cracked up to be by the do-gooders. Frank Lloyd Wright: "I had the opportunity a long time ago to choose between hypocritical humility and honest arrogance, and I chose the latter and have never regretted it."

Yet when we focus on our legacy—that which we're handing down to others—we become overwhelmingly humble. We lose our scientific certainty, we forget about the need for a world-class doctor, *and we put it off until the Judgment Day or End of Days and remove the focus.*

What Do You Mean, "What Do You Mean?"

We've dispensed "meaning" to those outer, dusty, insect-ridden bins in the basement of our minds. We're caught in a kaleidoscopic world where the shapes and colors never do coalesce or form patterns because we're not turning the cylinder.

Most people work, dine, and sleep. There is little time for play, unless it's relegated to a quick vacation, often hooked on to a business trip like a caboose on a freight train. There is even less time for understanding or insight, for exploration or growth. Our growth is programmed into our school years, when we actually went on field trips, were forced to read books we'd otherwise use as drink coasters, and interacted with diverse classmates.

Once we enter the workforce, blue collar, white collar, or no collar, we enter the ruts of life. Like cross-country skiing, we travel in ruts made by someone else as fast and expediently as possible. If we try to travel fast and find someone blocking us at a glacier pace, we're forced to move into other ruts to pass, if they are even available.

A recent study showed that current eighth graders are woefully inept in both history and geography. Small wonder with today's teaching emphasis. And it won't get any better in high school or college, where the political orientations of the professors trump learning. We no longer "school," we now indoctrinate. Our kids understand neither where they've come from nor where they are.

People can't use language properly, can't identify other countries on a map, can't tell you whether the American or Russian Revolution came first. So we dumb down our language, losing nuance, and dumb down our society with "casual everyday" at work. We've become exemplified by the guy with his baseball cap on backward using his hand to shield his face from the sun!

We don't really understand "meaning," from others or in nature. My definition of "spirituality" isn't religious, but rather one of connection. We too often look back in regret and look forward in dread, when we should be looking around in awareness. There will be more on this throughout the book.

I'm asked constantly, after 60+ books, where I get my material. (I tell people at first that I strive for volume and not accuracy, and about half, astoundingly, believe that on face value.) I reply that I merely look around. It's hard for me to look at my fellow humans and believe we're biological accidents. I don't think that animals are so inferior to us, not so long as the squirrels can figure out entry to any Fort Knox-like bird feeder, and my dogs are such effective groakers.*

The great naturalist John Muir was asked once the reason for poison ivy, since it did us no good and was potentially so irritating. "Why was it made?" was the inquiry.

"Perhaps," he said, "it was made for itself."

I find that people either assume what's meant without exploration, or simply chant, "What do you mean?" I told a coaching client that he might have excellent methodology, but that this was the marketing business and he wasn't appearing on prospects' radar screens.

"What do you mean?" he asked.

I told him that he was creating intellectual property in splendid isolation, an artist who was in a room with his own work wondering why the public didn't appreciate it.

"What do you mean?" Apparently, it was Groundhog Day.

---

* An old Scottish term meaning "to stare at someone else's food in the hopes of being given some."

"YOU NEED TO FIND YOUR APPROPRIATE BUYERS AND GET IN FRONT OF THEM TO MARKET YOUR TALENTS AND OFFERINGS!"

"Why are you shouting?" he asked.

There are thousands of comic panels depicting people seeking the guru, the fount of knowledge, who can explain succinctly and coherently what the hell we're doing here and what we should be pursuing. The hard-wired belief is that we have to find something, like those strange people walking deserted beaches at 6 am with metal detectors and ear phones, searching for lost items of worth. I doubt that any one of them has ever found anything that has paid for the equipment.

How many good books could they have read, or good deeds they could have done, or great love they could have expressed in all that time, instead of looking to gain from others' losses?

Life is not a search for meaning provided by someone else. Figure 1.1 depicts the stereotypical mountain climbed to find the guru who tells you what you already know (or what could be in a fortune cookie.) All the great religions maintain that there are ideal ways to conduct yourself—tolerance and forgiveness being pretty good basic ideas—but even the Ten Commandments are largely "shalt nots" and not "shalts."

If the quest is futile, then what's the point about living and life?

Meaning Within

Creating meaning from within begins with our beliefs, values, and consequent self-identity. We rarely focus on these, even though they tend to guide us unconsciously and viscerally every day. Unless we are in a traumatic circumstance (as we were with the pandemic), or in therapy (often as the result of a traumatic circumstance), we have very little opportunity to examine, or even identify and articulate these gyroscopes.

Beliefs are those logical thoughts and rationality (be they true or false, though we think they're true) that create acceptance and conviction. This is

Figure 1.1 *Seeking the guru.*

from the Constitution of the United States, though in many schools you'd never know it today:

> *We hold these truths to be self-evident, that all men are created equal, that they are endowed by their Creator with certain unalienable rights...*

The problem, of course, is that this was written when slavery was in full blossom in America, and Jefferson, the author of these mighty words, was a slaveholder who also wrote (about slavery):

> *I tremble for my country when I reflect that God is just.*

Sometime later, the "three-fifths compromise" determined that slaves would be counted as three-fifths of whites when determining a state's population, which determined its number of representatives.

"We believe that all men are created equal" isn't as "self-evident" as the grand phrase implies, since it doesn't say "all white men" and it doesn't say "not counting black men or women of all kinds."

Thus, our beliefs aren't always borne out in objective truth, even though others may hold those same beliefs. That is, they may guide our behavior but they may not be ethically or even empirically true.

We believed, when I was young, that going into the ocean within an hour of eating a meal would cause severe cramps which could lead to drowning. We actually sat on the beach, with our parents' blessing, counting down the minutes, as if even the final 90 seconds could mean the difference between life and death.

As I write this some people believe that the coronavirus was weaponized by China, that there is a United Nations conspiracy to take over the world, that dead aliens from space are being hidden by the government, and that vaccinating children against measles might well trigger autism. None of these beliefs is supported by evidence or facts, but they nonetheless influence behavior and create meaning for many people.

Of course, many people also have beliefs that we should help the less fortunate, comply with rules for the common good, and that charity isn't about how much one gives but rather how much one has left *after* one gives.

Our country continues to examine its beliefs through a free press and contested elections of candidates who express varied positions. *But we don't have such mechanisms for ourselves.*

Beliefs obviously can and should change when appropriate, when learning occurs, as maturity grows. My beliefs about capital punishment changed from "for" to "against" in the latter stages of my life.

Values denote principles and standards of behaviors. They imply the worth of something. Our values include issues such as proper behavior in various circumstances, individual rights, health, family, financial well-being, and so forth.

Values are often affected by normative pressure, that is, the tendency of peers to influence what one believes. The way we dress and attempt to impress others, the music we listen to, the cars we drive are all manifestations of the importance we place on "fitting in" or "being part of the right crowd." A vast number of sociological studies have found that people tend to choose to live in areas with people of like values.

Case Study: Diana

We were at my wife's 30th college reunion and her classmate Diana arrived by herself, decked out in her best finery. My wife explained that, after 24 years of marriage, Diana had recently divorced. I had met her when my wife and I were dating ages ago. She still looked stunning.

My wife instructed me in that long-time-marriage-whisper, "Ask her to dance!" I don't dance well, so I waited for a slow song since I'm capable of rocking back and forth with an attractive woman in my arms.

After a minute of awkward silence, I mined my limited social language skills enough to ask, "How are you doing?" Diana interpreted this to means "since the divorce."

"Not so good," she admitted. "It's been less than a year."

Now socially operating on fumes, I asked this: "When did you know it wasn't working?"

"After the first year," she said.

I stopped rocking.

"You have to realize," she explained, "we're Italian, my parents wanted grandchildren, I couldn't leave."

I wept in her hair.

However, extreme peer influence can distort or override values. This is often called the threshold principle. An upstanding citizen whose values respect law and order, finding himself or herself in the middle of a riot, might well loot a store because everyone around is doing so. A brave soldier might flee if all others in the unit are fleeing, or a scared soldier might stay instead of fleeing since all comrades are staying.

The accumulation of values creates meaning, yet we seldom tap into these values formally, let alone change or examine them. You value the relationships in your family, but they sometimes must change because of alienation, addiction, abandonment, criminality or brutality. Many people remain in marriages far too long, as did Diana, because their unexamined value is that they would disappoint too many people by leaving, yet they do far more harm to themselves and others by staying.

Many of our values are not only unspoken, but subconscious and subliminal.

Vision is a mental panorama of what the future might look like. There are generic visions, encapsulated in metaphors such as "the American Dream" wherein everyone has a chance to be wealthy, healthy, and wise. (As in Tevye's lament in "If I Were A Rich Man"—"When you're rich they think you *really know*.") Especially in our youth, our vision is of near-immortality and it's just a matter of time until blazing success occurs.

There are more personalized visions, of course. We meet people who have wanted to become, since a very young age, a classical cellist, or thoracic surgeon, or major league pitcher, or fire fighter, or diplomat. The problem is that too often the vision is in place for the wrong reasons. The dentist's child becomes a dentist without any passion for the calling.* The grocer's child takes over the family business as an obligation. The child admires a nurse (or a teacher or an actor) and vows to become one.

Our vision needs to be examined and refined as we grow. Otherwise, we have a very strong wind propelling us to the wrong destination. If you don't know your port-of-call, no wind is a good wind.

---

* Dentists and psychologists have two of the highest rates of professional suicide in the country. Psychologists because they enter the profession already troubled and are trying to heal themselves; dentists because the job is routine and boring with high debt and not easily transportable. No pun intended, but the dentist is "rooted" to the community.

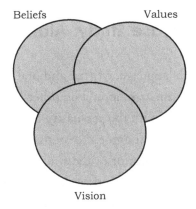

Beliefs and values but no vision: Lost at sea, no port insight
Values and vision but no beliefs: Lack of navigation
Vision and beliefs but no values: Sinking, no integrity in the craft

Figure 1.2   *Beliefs, values, and vision.*

As you can see in Figure 1.2, creating meaning for yourself on the way to establishing legacy requires a conscious effort to examine these three elements. But we don't operate in a vacuum. Let's see what influences on meaning are occurring around us.

Meaning Without

There are forces around us (I described normative pressures above) which also determine meaning for us. Sometimes we recognize them, as in political platforms or choosing our friends, but sometimes they are totally subliminal, as in hidden environmental influences.

Do you remember in the early days of television that some people claimed subconscious messages were between the flickers on the screen? Or that some records and recordings held demonic messages revealed at different speeds? Hypnosis, after all, is real and medically practiced by some therapists to "dig out" hidden meanings harbored in the recesses of our brains.

Of course, sometimes a more insidious "hypnosis" plants them there.

Case Study: Alan

I was always great with language, written and oral, and could influence arguments even in grammar school. The other kids might have been "right," but I was the one with the persuasive language. (As the lawyers say, depressingly, "If you can't argue the merits, argue the law.")

In high school I became editor of the student newspaper and president of the student council. Everyone either told me or assumed that I should be a lawyer, a profession at the time much more admired than today. They didn't see me in bizarre personal injury advertisements on television, but rather as a trial lawyer romancing a jury.

At Rutgers, I majored in political science, a natural precursor to law. And when I took the LSATs, I crushed them. Rutgers Law, a great school, offered me a full scholarship, which was the jackpot for a kid from a family with no money.

That summer, after graduation, it hit me like that meteor hit the Yucatan that I didn't want to be a lawyer. I hated detail work, detested research, was bored by contracts, and both running my own practice (for which I had no money) and joining a partner track at a ginormous firm with 80-hour weeks (for which I had no stomach) were equally repugnant.

I went to the Dean of the Law School Admissions in Newark and explained that she could give the scholarship to someone else, I was going to go get a job. She stood up, reached across the desk and tried to grab my wrist, yelling, "But you ought to be a lawyer!"

I ran out into the streets and never looked back.

The external influences on our interpretation of "meaning" and our formulation and reformulation of it are vaster than they've ever been. They include:

• Parents' instructions, behaviors, opinions, friends, and careers
• Teachers' apparent behavior and subtle behavior*

---

* This includes political commentary, social reactions, respect for institutions, and so forth.

- Siblings, particularly older ones presumably more experienced
- Social interactions and close friends
- Experience with institutions and businesses
- Financial reality of well-being or threat
- Social media opinion and their tropism toward confirmation bias
- Competition and rivalries, perceived "enemies"
- Political platforms and "causes"
- Participation sports
- Sources of non-scholastic learning
- Trauma: death of loved ones, illness, threats, accidents, mistakes

"Meaning" begins to lose its meaning under this barrage of sound and fury. The beliefs, values, and vision described earlier were often cast or at least formed by three elements:

- Family dinner table, where young people learned of the realities of life and how to handle the vicissitudes thereof. Even if the outcomes weren't helpful or successful, there was learning about what beliefs and values guided the discussion. The family dinner table has become virtually extinct, a stegosaurus of experiences, with the two-income family, extracurricular activities, non-intact homes, and the lures of the internet.
- Religious institutions, where beliefs are paramount, and the manifestation of those beliefs in correct behavior was constantly preached, often with the threat of sin and hell appertaining. This source was compromised by the horrid pedophilia of priests and cover-ups by bishops, by the anti-religionists implications that religion is for the mentally backward, and by a refusal by youth to conform to such discipline and time requirements.*

---

* It is interesting, however, how many people who abjure services routinely return to have their children baptized, to marry, and to bury their family members. There is apparently a "meaning" in that belief system that is too strong to be totally undermined.

- Educational institutions were to provide the intellectual arena in which young people could argue beliefs, challenge values, and hone visions. However, these have changed into bastions of political correctness, inhibitors of speech not in vogue with the faculty and administration, and bullying environments where "if you're not with us you're against us." The traditional American liberal arts education has all but disappeared.

The abdication or loss of these engines for the discovery of meaning have had a huge, deleterious impact on people's lives, self-worth, and control. The default mechanism has become business, which is singularly poorly designed to deal with these dynamics. By the time young people reached their first job they were supposed to have been inculcated with certain beliefs, values, and vision: What's important, what's correct, and what's my share of The Dream?

Instead, they arrive barely literate enough to write a business memo.

Let's go on to explore what these foundations of meaning have to do with our legacy, both individually and collectively.

CHAPTER 2

The Ritual of Competition

There are origins of competitiveness that are no longer valid but which continue to influence us. What difference does it make standing up first to retrieve overhead baggage in a plane parked at the gate after landing? We compete about inconsequential things, often unaware of our own actions. Yet there are times when appropriate competition is a great reconciler and consensus builder. But what are the boundaries? Our legacy is too often tied to others' (often dysfunctional) behaviors.

Why We're So Damn Competitive

I remarked to one of my best, most successful coaching clients that she is highly competitive, almost as competitive as I am.

"I'm much more competitive than you are!!" she shouted.

Why do we compete so much?

While the word itself often invokes negative emotions such as jealousy, the "rat race," and doing anything to get ahead, competition is a natural human condition. We may not be competing for food or ideal caves any more, but we are nonetheless in some competitive situations.

I've always thought that it was a sign of health to be competitive. And, after all, we're often competing with ourselves to do better than last time, to break our own "records," to finish sooner than expected. But even in competition with others, whether the other party knows it or not, these aren't discriminatory emotions or acts.

The term "arriviste" is applied to people who are ruthless in seeking their own ends, social status, and wealth. I'm not referring to that level of competition here. Competing in a healthy way—not to have the biggest, or fastest, or the most expensive, but merely to attain what makes you fulfilled—means that you have to overcome several obstacles.

Rumors and gossip tend to distort what we're trying to accomplish because other people don't understand our metrics (they are using their own) or they are threatened by us. People tend to resent others who are more successful, at best calling them "lucky" and at worst "devious."

We create self-denial when we are threatened by the comments of others (or perceived potential comments) and lie to ourselves that we really don't want or need what we were considering. Do I really need a new car? Not if the neighbors are offended by thinking I'm better than they are.

We use the wrong metrics, so we think we should compete for what others are seeking, yet our hearts aren't in it and we're doomed to fail. A successful entrepreneur asked me what kind of luxury car she should consider since all of her peers were buying them. "Do you even like cars?" I asked. "Actually no," she said, "and I rarely drive." Well, fuggeddaboudit.

The chart in Figure 2.1 is a representation of psychologist Abraham Maslow's famous "hierarchy of needs."[*] On the lowest level we have traditionally always had to compete for basic sustenance, and as we progress upwards we do find ourselves competing for security, friends, love, and prestige.

Even at Maslow's highest level we unfortunately tend to compete for leaving the largest impression on the world, for the greatest impact in our surroundings, for the most profound *legacy*.

And this, may I say heretically, is where Maslow is wrong. (His hierarchy has never been scientifically proven or validated, and I believe people tend to jump up and down through the levels as their lives and circumstances

---

[*] From https://www.simplypsychology.org/maslow.html.

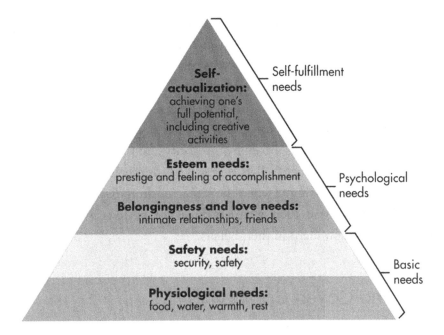

Figure 2.1 *Maslow's hierarchy of needs.*

change.) There comes a time when competition has to be assessed in order for it to make sense.

Competition for success: This may be outperforming others in order to achieve a job, an assignment, tenure, funding, election, and other such accomplishments important for our careers, relationships, and health.

Competition for fun: This would include anything from athletics to board games, from writing something before someone else does, to solving a Rubik's Cube faster than others. (I have never been able to do that.) I read of an executive who flushed the toilet before he urinated, and then competed to see if he could finish relieving himself before the flush ended. There are even targets you can float in the toilet bowl. (But, I digress.)

Competition for ego: You want to get tickets to the hot Broadway play, or to the Super Bowl, or get the finest suite on the cruise ship, or get the best seat in the restaurant. There's nothing wrong with this *unless you are upset and/or seek vengeance if you don't "win" that competition*. It's fine to stand in line from 5 am, but it's not so fine if you try to cut the line.

Competition for competition's sake: this is the real toxin. Microsoft co-founder Paul Allen and the Sultan of Brunei aren't constantly building larger yachts for any of the above reasons, they're simply two guys with way too much money who are trying to buy one-upsmanship. I believe this is the cause of religious animosity (or atheist/religious enmity) because one side can't simply allow the other to believe in what it chooses and to co-exist. This kind of competition is driven by insecurity and low self-esteem. People who turn violent when their beliefs are mocked (or even satirized) have inferiority complexes. You'll note when the rather scathing *Book of Mormon* was produced on Broadway, there were no threats or protests by the Mormon Church. They're confident in their beliefs.

Overt and Covert Competing

We compete overtly—openly—much more frequently than we believe, or let on. Competition is about "rivalry," and not all rivalry is bad. (We're talking about "rivals," not necessarily "enemies.") Competition creates an adrenaline rush, and helps us meet deadlines and perform well under pressure.

Some people will not enter a competition if they believe they can't win. This severely limits their ability to succeed. You have to "call for the ball" for the winning shot. But you can't score if you're not on the court.

Moreover, competition is not a zero-sum game. For us to win, no one else must necessarily lose. That's a common misconception, but in business we often hear of win/win situations where everyone comes out ahead (the whole is greater than the sum of the parts). I've always coached that for partnerships and collaborations to work, 1 + 1 can't equal 2, it has to equal about 64.

Here's why overt, unabashed, unashamed, focused competition is good for your health, good for your soul, and creates legacy for you daily:

1. We're forced to be more innovative. To "win" requires that we either do things better than others or, preferably, create new standards of

success which others can't meet. Thus, we're no longer merely problem solvers who restore performance to old levels when something goes wrong.

2. Our values change. We see ourselves in a better light, generate more confidence, improve our self-esteem, use more positive self-talk. We become accustomed to competing well and winning often, and that becomes self-reinforcing.

3. Our resilience grows. I've found resilience—rebounding from setbacks and defeats and disappointments better than ever—to improve substantially when we fail to win in a competitive event *rather than never engage in it at all.* We actually learn how better to win by watching others and/or by examining our own performance.

4. It clears our heads. We have clear goals—the result of the competition—and we're focused on where we're going. We aren't so easily distracted and we stop procrastinating.

5. Our perspective improves. "Success is never final and failure seldom fatal," said Churchill, and we understand how to be gracious losers *and gracious winners.* We don't irritate others in our arrogance, and we don't wallow in despair in our loses.

6. We're perceived as "players." We're seen as people who are in the hunt, in the major leagues, serious about our pursuits. We're bold enough, skilled enough, and talented enough to be in the fray.

We have to change our mindset from "competitive" as pejorative to "competitive" as healthy. I don't think anyone would feel that Jack Welch, Tiger Woods, Lady Gaga, Tom Brady, Selena Williams, or Steve Jobs was or is "overly competitive." We tend to think of these people as winners, more often than not.

Covert competing is a different animal.

People can readily, secretly compete with you (as you can with them). I'm reminding you in terms of life's meaning and legacy that healthy competition is essential. But it's not good to compare ourselves to someone else's legacy, someone else's metrics, someone else's standards. This is *unhealthy* competition, and it's often not easily seen or realized.

Healthy competition involves the hard work and discipline to be effective and succeed. But unhealthy competition implies that others must fail in order for you to succeed.

Here are the signs that someone may be "out to get you" or that, despite your own disclaimers, you are out to get them.

1. Boasting. Exaggeration of achievements and constant reference to them. This is most likely when the other person (the "target") is receiving recognition or acclaim.

2. Passive aggressiveness. This is a subtle undermining through promises unkept and deadlines unmet, procrastination, and damning with false praise. (You had an excellent round of golf today but, of course, nothing compared to your older sister.)

3. Questioning success. These are suggestions that the competition was weak, or you were lucky, or the goals weren't all that hard. Sometimes they simply ignore the success altogether, as if it never happened.

4. Rumor and innuendo. "He was promoted because he doesn't threaten the boss with his skills," or "She received the award because they hadn't offered it to a woman in several years."

5. They "enter the picture." This is like "photo bombing" but in a movie, not a snapshot. Your success finds the other person somehow involved though they were never otherwise present or helpful. They are taking a small (or large) share of the credit that should be yours alone.

6. False interest. People want to know how you are and what's going on, what progress you're making. They want to know what they need to be preparing for or perhaps undermining in the near future.

7. They celebrate your defeats. The mock the poor showing, they claim they had predicted it, they generalize it into your overall incompetence instead of a singular setback.

8. They rally others against you. They find kindred "silent competitors" to form a bloc against you and minimize your successes while maximizing your failures (or inventing them).

9. They "become you." The emulate what you do and often claim that they wrote, or achieved, or said something before you did, even if blatantly untrue.

10. They create dangerous challenges. They will seemingly praise your success but then challenge you with an unachievable goal, as if to prove that you can do anything while knowing you'll fail.

11. Sabotage. Mail isn't received, calls aren't returned, email is misdirected, meeting times are changed. You're made to look incompetent through deliberate acts of malice that are readily deniable.

Create valuable meaning and a positive, memorable legacy. Don't let people do this to you, but also don't allow yourself to do this to others. Covert competition is unhealthy and malicious.

Societal Benefits and the Healing of the High Jump

We can create meaning in healthy competition that transcends the mere act of competing. A relay team must gracefully and affirmatively pass the baton to each member in order to win the race. We keep track of "assists" in basketball and hockey, and there is something balletic about a double play in baseball. We admire a good block in football often as much as the runner it sets free.

We generally prize teamwork in business, as well. We're forever "team building" (even though almost all organizations have committees and not teams).* We're proud to chant that "there is no 'I' in 'team,'" though we seem to overlook the fact that there *is* one in "win."

---

* A team is of equals who win and lose together and consequently share resources, information, budgets—whatever it takes. They help the weakest member across the finish line together. A committee comprises diverse interests who may share with other members so long as it doesn't hinder personal accomplishment, and some members can "win" while others "lose." The weakest members are usually left by the wayside.

Nevertheless, there are tremendous societal benefits in healthy competition and open competition. Consider this, for example:

"Two old men. Enemies who spoke different languages and couldn't even agree on a way to prevent the world from blowing up. Yet there they were, embracing like brothers on world television at the simple act of a man jumping over a bar."

This was spoken by legendary sports producer Roone Arledge (who originated "Monday Night Football"), cited as the most important thing he ever broadcast, which was Nikita Khrushchev and US Assistant Secretary of State Averell Harriman celebrating Russia's Valery Brumel's record high jump at the 1963 Olympics.

Healthy people tend to root even for the competition. Gracious stars in entertainment, athletics, and the arts tend to salute others' victories. There are traditions of "jumping the net" to honor the winner of the tennis match, or of basketball and hockey players shaking everyone's hand in line at the end of a game (which is a tradition at the Little League World Series, as well).

Of course, we see the dysfunction in fields such as politics. Despite the usual (though not always) support of the winner by the rivals for the office, during the contest the competition is beyond ugly and acrimonious. As I write this, Joe Biden has named Kamala Harris as his vice-presidential choice, though in the primary debates she implied he was a racist.

There is an old, tired parable about a visitor seeing construction underway and asking a laborer what he is doing.

"I'm laying bricks," he replies.

A bit farther on, the visitor asks another laborer the same question, and this one replies, "I'm building a cathedral."

The point is supposed to be that we are best engaged when looking at the goal of our work (or life) and not at specific tasks. But I've always felt the story is incomplete and not even understood.

There should be a third inquiry with another laborer who says, "I'm bringing people closer to God."

There is a job, a career, and then there's a *calling*. Our legacy is about our calling and about the role of our healthy competitiveness in realizing that calling. That high jump took place in the Olympics which, in modern times, has tried to symbolize healthy international competition which transcends geopolitical boundaries, ethnicities, and ancient animosities. Sportswriter Grantland Rice is purported to have observed, "It doesn't matter whether you win or lose, it's how you play the game."

However, even with lofty goals, the Olympics keeps track of which countries have the most medals and plays the national anthem of the winning country after every event. And we have doping scandals and gender challenges and athletes representing countries in which they don't live and, perhaps, have never even visited.

I think the Olympics are a nice try, and that high jump record during the height of the Cold War was an example of healthy competition that can, however briefly, trump the hostility of harsh adversaries and differing philosophies of government and freedom. Thus, we have some precedent, some inkling, of the contribution of healthy competition.

One of the problems we face today is with the "coddled generation" which refers to that cohort of youth which requires "trigger warnings" at school in case something about to be read or discussed might be somehow damaging to their psyches. They receive "participation awards" for merely showing up and not for excellence in competitive games or competitive educational contests, such as essays or debates or research papers. We've done away in many schools with valedictorians and "top ten" lists in scholastic achievement. We've turned to "pass/fail" instead of actual grades (the cognate being "gradation" which shows varying degrees of success).

I've seen boards of non-profits elect offices not based on experience or intelligence or credentials, but rather on the basis that "everyone should have a chance." Perhaps everyone should have a chance in the sandbox or playing with communal toys, but not at flying the plane, unless you have the experience, aptitude, and certifications.

Otherwise, you can kill people.

Are we raising our kids with the right competitive spirit to not merely survive but to exceed—to thrive—in a highly competitive world?

Canadian geese, which are protected in the US under the Migratory Aquatic Wildlife Law, or some crazy legislation, are not migratory. Most stay in the US, so they must have the visa thing figured out. They tend to return to raise young where they were raised, such as on our property, and they mate for life. We have scores of geese here every year, and average 6–20 goslings. This year we have 12. The geese are nasty in protecting the kids (in fact, unlike all other Canadians, they are nasty pretty much all of the time and will even try to run after my cars), and one was killed one year when it stupidly tried to take on Koufax, our German Shepherd. But they do routinely fight off predators like raccoons and foxes.

In any case, at this time of year, all the parents gather all the kids down at our bridge about 100 yards away, and teach them to fly by first "walking on the water" and then lifting off, landing near our pool on the other end of the pond. This happens for less than a week and the young are soon flying. Then they leave to start their own independent lives, having been raised in safe conditions, with ample food and protection.

As nasty as they are, these geese are great parents. They mate for life, raise, educate, and protect their kids, and teach them how to survive in a competitive world.

Kind of frightening that they're better than we are at this.

The Point of No Return

The ritual of competition is ingrained from the dusty ancestry of survival. People competed with their prey, competed with each other for access to resources, competed over mates, and so forth. The fact that we do this over similar issues today is no surprise, but the fact that we've extended it to rather trivial pursuits is astonishing.

We've all seen the "sore loser" who throws a racket or hurls a tantrum, blaming the officials, the conditions, or the fates. But there are also sore winners who feel they haven't won by enough or, worse, it's insufficient to win and the other party must also "lose."

Thus, we have polarization and moral narcissism. These are closely related.

Polarization is the refusal to lessen harshly opposing positions. There is no room for compromise *because I am right and, therefore, you have to be wrong.* Once upon a time we hailed "great compromisers" in our government, who could cross party lines and attract those of opposing views. This isn't restricted to any one party. Bill Clinton won over Independents and Republicans, and Ronald Reagan won over Independents and Democrats. One of the reasons that Hillary Clinton lost to Donald Trump in a huge upset in 2016 was that her campaign *assumed* that virtually *all* women, and *all* blue-collar workers, and *all* union members, and *all* minorities would vote for her.

But that's not what happened. Many of them voted instead to be free of a "tribe" that was demanding uniformity.

Moral narcissism is the belief that one's opinions emanate from a higher moral plain. It is not just a position of greater rationality, or greater intellect, *it is a superior moral position.* Hence, there is no room for compromise because there is no room for descending to an inferior ethical level.

And thus we have "the point of no return." Our beliefs and causes and agendas become ossified, rigid, and unbending. We don't look at a candidate's platform, we look only for the candidate's stance on our single agenda item, because that item sets us apart on a higher level of purity.

We've all witnessed the bedlam that breaks lose when a plane lands and reaches the gate. The pilot signals with a bell that we can rise, and everyone leaps to their feet to pull down the overhead luggage. This occurs despite the fact that the plane door won't open for another five or more minutes, that many people will have to wait at baggage claim anyway, or that no one in the back is getting out before the people in the front unless they take the emergency exits.

I've giddily watched people maneuver in line to get close to an escalator on a crowded train platform, or an opening elevator in a hotel lobby. In

England and Japan, it's proper to queue up at certain positions to board a train. In the US it looks more like a rugby scrum.

We surreptitiously but obviously hand *maître d*'s cash in order to jump a line or get the best table. At immigration, entering a country, or a toll booth on a highway, we jump around trying to save five seconds. Our competition has reached hilarious but often dysfunctional levels.

Am I overreacting? Consider what we call "road rage." Someone commits a (usually) innocent error by cutting someone off or tailgating, and another driver takes it as a personal affront, a pre-meditated attack on their character. They retaliate not innocently, and cause another overreaction. In too many cases this escalates into a violent act: People are beaten up and even killed. In one case in Rhode Island when the two occupants emerged from their vehicles one of them took a crossbow out of his trunk and shot and killed the other. In New York, an enraged driver walked to the other driver's car, pulled her small dog out of the passenger seat, and threw it in front of an oncoming truck, killing it instantly. These are not isolated incidents.

The problem becomes one of legacy when you consider the fact that many people are in a permanent state of "life rage." Life rage characteristics are:

- Assuming the other person has evil and malicious intent.
- Seeing all setbacks and critique as personal attacks.
- Possessing a moral narcissism and believing you're better than everyone else.
- Never being willing for forgive or forget, and holding grudges.
- Believing in conspiracies and generally being paranoid.
- Blaming all problems on others and never accepting personal accountability.

To counteract life rage, since many of us enter it only sporadically and can emerge again, consider two facts:

1. We must judge an adverse impact on us caused by others in terms of its intent. Did my spouse hide the remote control to prevent me from

watching the start of my favorite program, or did she simply forget to put it back in the holder, as I often do myself?

2. When we hold someone else responsible—hold a grudge, seek a vendetta—*and they don't realize it, we are controlled by them.* Someone who is unaware the we perceive they've caused us harm can never apologize or "undo" something they're no longer concerned about (or don't believe ever happened).

Hence, we reach a point of no return when we place ourselves in a position without remediation, one in which we can't emerge because the remedy is no longer available or the damage is perceived as too great to our psyches.

Our competitive nature is fine, if controlled and directed toward our success and not a zero-sum game in which you must lose in order for me to win. Overt competing, with clear metrics and rules and a healthy attitude, builds character and success. Covert competing usually is dysfunctional, and creates a perpetual feeling of incompletion and non-success. The societal (and personal and business) benefits of competition *are only achieved so long as everyone recognizes the rules and abides by them, and is a healthy winner and healthy non-winner.*

"Participation trophies" for merely showing up are justifiably mocked, but congratulations for doing one's best even in a losing cause should also be lauded.

Now let's take a look at why "size" really doesn't matter.

CHAPTER 3

The Superficiality of Size

Size is often a disadvantage (try to parallel park an SUV), and strength today is not totally reliant on human muscle. The "super fit" and the careful dieters are often those who drop from heart attacks in the streets. Our advertising and corporate promotion are often unconsciously directed to the wrong appeal. Our legacy shouldn't be "nth" or "est." Why do we praise miniaturization and agility in some aspects (microchips, sports cars) but believe we need a 20-room mansion to be comfortable, or food hanging off our plates to enjoy a good meal?

Why Is Bigger or Faster or Cheaper Better?

Sinatra used to sing a song called, "I'd Like to Get You on A Slow Boat to China," the implications of which are pretty obvious. Despite the "mile high" club, you can't do what he's suggesting on a 787. (At least not comfortably or in duration.)

There are applicable parables, of course, from the turtle and the hare to the grasshopper and the ants. We hear about "measuring twice and cutting once." Then there's "slow and steady does it." And we frequently tell everyone to "take your time, what's the rush?"

Paul Allen and the Sultan of Brunei referred to earlier are examples of two guys just trying to have the biggest boat. Yet, I tell people all the time in a phrase I've coined: TIAABB. There is *always a bigger boat*. What's the sense of having something bigger than you need?

Or faster? My Corvette ZO6, a seven-speed manual, is rated at about 2.9 seconds from zero to sixty, but its governor holds the car to 150 MPH. I'll never need to go anywhere near even 150, nor to accelerate under three seconds to 60 MPH. I drive the Vette for the fun of steering and shifting on winding roads, and can barely get the Vette into seventh gear so I'm certainly not lobbying for eight.

Yet we prize restaurants that heap half a cow on the plates, and delight in "all you can eat" buffets. People on cruise ships seldom see the water because they're jamming their mouths with anything not nailed down throughout the day.

I've watched people in theaters prize themselves on seats close to the stage until someone 6'6" sits immediately in front of them. The folks up in the balconies have better views.

Our legacy needn't be about the "greatest" and the "most" and the "finest." It should be about contribution and love and lasting impressions. I was never impressed by the *amount* of vacation photos I was shown (though often bored to tears) but I have been impressed by the *quality and character* of such photos. The "best" people in sports are often not really the best people in life (legendary coach Vince Lombardi was a horrible husband and father, for example; baseball great Ty Cobb was a commonly acknowledged "dirty player").

People seek to dive deeper into the ocean depths to find creatures never before witnessed by humans, yet we don't take the time to observe and enjoy the beauty of nature around us. We've substituted arbitrary metrics for deep understanding. We want to build and drive cars that can go faster than ever on a track, but don't understand where we are in the universe.

Whether you use religious teachings to try to create a meaning, or scientific teachings to try to organize what we know (which is very little), we are simply using excuses for our ignorance. (Are the stories of Genesis and the Big Bang Theory really vastly different?) We try to organize all around us, even the infinity of space, so as not to grapple with the metaphysical issues about why we're here, and what is our purpose. We proudly teach youngsters about metamorphosis in caterpillars and photosynthesis in plants, 17-year cicadas and wonderfully extinct ancient life forms, but we don't apply such amazements metaphorically to our own lives.

I reiterate that our legacy is about *creating meaning* for ourselves and others. It's not about a search for something, as if meaning has been discovered and was hushed up, or lost down a sewer. I'd like to think that our legacies are truly about questioning our role, our calling, our relationships with the world around us.

We had both an egret and a heron on our pond not long ago, both regular visitors. An osprey also flew in. I don't need to explore to see if we have fish in the pond, because the birds wouldn't be here if we didn't. They're not just sightseeing or taking a break. They're looking for their lunch or maybe their family's dinner.

We don't make sufficient deductions like that. We just see birds and wonder if we have fish. We see high-performing people and low-performing people and try to assess blame for the discrepancy instead of finding cause. And we create the damned arbitrary metrics to keep us happy: Rhode Island has two schools considered head and shoulders above all others in the state. But neither is in the top 100 nationally. So how good can they be? Compared to what? A broken clock is correct twice a day.

My point is not that you have to be the best. My point is that your effort has to be the best you're capable of giving.

Festivus and Feats of Strength

Festivus is an alternative, secular holiday to Christmas celebrated on December 23 and created by author Daniel O'Keefe in 1966 with his family, but popularized on the comedy show *Seinfeld* in 1997. The celebrations include a bare aluminum pole, the airing of grievances, miracles (which aren't so miraculous), and feats of strength.

While absolutely hysterical as performed on the show and wonderfully ludicrous as the venture seems, why is it any different from any other holiday?

Christmas, that religious-cum-secular celebration of global impact, is hugely competitive, from the "Black Friday" prior to Christmas wherein sales cause people to gather at 3 am to rush the doors at 6 am and brawls and invective are the order of the day. The frenzied competition includes the nature of the presents, the largest tree, the best ornaments, the most food, and most drunks. And I remind you of the traffic-jamming, million-light extravaganzas that people (and, often, entire neighborhoods) erect on their property.

Christmas, while not the holiest tradition in Christianity (which is Easter), is supposed to be the enjoyment of the birth of the Savior. Instead it has become the beginning of an orgy of gifts, food, and booze, with the aforementioned airing of grievances usually filling the night. But it's not even over then, because the "holiday season" culminates in New Year's with over a million people gathering in urban drunken stupors to watch a ball fall and then watch each other fall. If Christmas is excess, New Year's is completely over-the-top.

Now, consider this all really begins in the US with Thanksgiving, and the greatest turkey, and the most stuffing, and the greatest number of courses, *ad nauseum*, and you have approximately seven weeks of grimly competitive celebration, from fireplaces to fireworks. And the arguments, the vitriol, among family members on these occasions are predictable and repetitive.

So I ask you, is Festivus really so silly or fictional?

Bristol, Rhode Island, has the longest-running Fourth of July parade in the US. *The Guinness Book of Records* does nothing but note the highest, lowest, shortest, farthest, fastest, and slowest. There is an annual hot dog eating contest in Coney Island covered by the major media. The largest commercial aircraft is the Airbus A-380 (I've been on some with showers on board) and the wingspan is longer than the Wright brothers' first flight. But that airplane's production has been reduced and will be halted in the near future according to current Airbus statements.

We don't always need the "est" and the "nth."

Our legacy is too often embroiled in feats of strength (and the airing of grievances). Our tendency is to "outdo" and "outperform." Even in acts of charity we indulge in competitive games, such as the "ice bucket challenge" for ALS disease in the recent past.

We need to stop celebrating competition and start celebrating accomplishment. Otherwise, we can't "win enough." We're told, "You did well, but not up to expectation," or "not up to the national top ten percent," or "not as well as your sister." That's a heavy burden and it becomes demoralizing and depressing.

Ask yourself *why* you're engaged in competition and Festivus-like activities. What is it that drives you to mindless competitiveness? Some solutions:

- Don't store up perceived slights in your cheeks like a chipmunk. Confront problems and unhappiness at the time they occur. Create a temporary unpleasantness in the confrontation that will prevent long-term pain and stress. Ask why you were omitted, and tell someone they have the story wrong, or confront rude behavior.
- Fight it or forget it. The "fight" doesn't need to be physical. Write a letter to the editor, contribute money to the opposition, avoid being in the same room, call them out. Or, don't do any of that and get on with your life. Otherwise, you'll internalize the stress and make yourself feel even worse than the perceived affront did.
- Look for middle ground. Billy Joel sings in "Shades of Grey" about "not being so sure anymore." We live in a polarized world, perhaps, but that doesn't mean that compromise and consensus don't exist and can't be employed. Let me remind you that consensus is something you can live with *and not something you'd die for.*
- Stop feeling as if you have to prove yourself to others (and particularly people newly met). People who trail initials after their names like ants attacking spilled food are classic cases of those who are so insecure that they have to "advertise" their credibility and credentials. Yet the more initials I see, the more suspicious I get. (I counted 19 initials I

could place after my name if I so chose, and all of that plus two dollars would get me on a bus.)

- Evaluate if it matters who "wins." If two people get on the escalator before I do, I don't resent my turn being taken. If people don't let me turn, I realize it's only a delay of about another minute. If someone gets the last of the meals I wanted on a flight I remind myself I'm not on the plane for the culinary experience.
- Go around the block. UPS teaches its drivers to make three right-hand turns to cross a street, rather than wait for one left turn against traffic. Don't take the escalator, use the stairs.

Drowning in Noise and Outrageousness

Have you ever experienced anyone on Facebook posting, "Thanks for your opinions and comments, you've changed my mind on this issue"? I haven't! The noise on Facebook is the clanging of the tribal gongs of moral narcissism. I'm not only right, but you're wrong and, moreover, I'm right because I occupy a higher moral position than you do. I will get to heaven, you won't.

Well, not if St. Peter is being objective, you won't.

There is tremendous normative pressure around us, forcing us to compromise our beliefs so that we don't compromise our affiliations. That, of course, is the exact reverse of what we should be doing. The "threshold principle" holds that good people will act in bad ways if everyone around them is. I arrived to protest, but my friends are also stealing computers. Although I think that's wrong, *everyone is doing it and I can use a new one.*

People use obscenities more when others in the conversation are doing so. People will change their stated positions not because they're convinced logically or rationally, but because they are seeking the affection and admiration of peers (not necessarily respect).

As you can see in Figure 3.1, when affiliation is high but respect is low we are "buddies." When both are low, we're just "suppliers" or vendors.

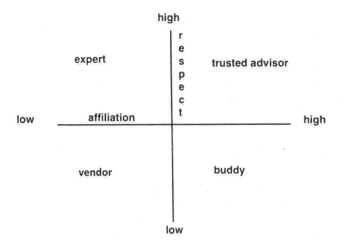

Figure 3.1 *Respect and affiliation.*

When respect is high but affiliation is low, we're seen as experts, perhaps distantly. When both are high, we're trusted. But we tend to "stop short" and simply seek affection and affiliation, meaning we're with the "in group" and subject to its norms.

I'd doubt that you'd want your legacy to be "She was a buddy in our in-group" or "He was always 'one of us'."

In this noise, we take refuge in biases:

- Confirmation bias: The tendency to listen and absorb only those ideas and opinions which reinforce our own, and to categorically reject those that do not.
- Recency bias: The tendency to listen to and act upon only what we've heard most recently, and not seek other input.
- Zero-sum bias: For me to win, you have to lose. For you to win, I have to lose. There is no win/win.
- Social desirability bias: The tendency to over-report positive traits about myself and to underreport those of others.*

---

* A popular, perhaps apocryphal, example is that 87 percent of Americans surveyed reported themselves as "above average" in intelligence.

- Selection bias: The tendency to be more aware of and sensitive to something that we're involved in. If we're buying a pickup truck we become more aware of pickup trucks.
- Normalcy bias: The tendency to be unprepared for and slow to act when something occurs not encountered ever before.
- Loudness bias: The tendency to react to whatever is making the most noise in order to stop it (the proverbial "squeaky wheel").

How do we extricate ourselves from these biases, which serve only to drown us in more noise and create even more outrageousness? Or is our legacy destined to be one of hiding in the herd, fleeing with the flock, submerging in the swarm?

We need to shed the need to be part of the "clique," the "in group," the "hip." If you want to wear a baseball cap backwards so you have to use your hand to shield your eyes from the sun, or wear enough bling around your neck to be a character in *The Sopranos*, then you might as well be in a school of fish. Get used to the water. No one is going to need a "bigger boat" (to quote the famous line in *Jaws*) when you appear. And even fish can die in the water if there isn't enough oxygen in it to sustain them.

How do we escape the noise and outrageousness?

- Free yourself from the need for affection from others (your family and close friends aren't "others"). Don't seek inclusion, seek evaluation. Are these people those with whom I share values (a community) or are they those whose values I'll be forced to accept to be included (a tribe)? We don't need immediate acceptance and love to lead our lives and create a legacy. If you do need unconditional love, then get a dog. I have two.
- Never believe something is inevitable, other than death. You aren't "predestined," in some Calvinistic universe, to be controlled by the fates. You have control over your decisions, responses, and emotions. It's not so much what happens to you in life, it's what you do about what happens to you.

- Utilize every experience as a learning and growth experience. Resilience is far more important than attempts at perfection. The latter "freezes" us and delays our actions until we think we're guaranteed success—which we never are. Perfectionism kills excellence. Resilience, however, enables us to learn from and grow with each setback and failure. There is no "win/loss" column. There is only life. Our legacy needs to be the result of that learning. Perfectionism fosters procrastination, while resilience creates results.

One Size Fits All!

Many of the organizations that were my Fortune 500 clients couldn't understand why "blanket" motivational programs (usually implemented by Human Resources people who were enthralled with some self-help book) didn't work well. Other firms implemented across-the-board "merit" pay increases, irrespective of the particular merit of any given performer. Even today, companies put their people, often at great expense, in a hall to hear a "motivational speaker."

The problem is that *there is no such thing as a "motivational speaker," because motivation is intrinsic.* It comes from within, not without.

One size doesn't fit all.

In fact, my experience shows that most people are motivated by agency, latitude for action, application of one's talents, and recognition for the results thus developed. Money is not a motivator (though its absence can be a demotivator—psychologist Fred Herzberg revealed this 70 years ago). If you give an unhappy employee more money, you merely create a wealthier unhappy employee.

As I write this, there are expensive commercials on television during prime time for socks. That's right: socks. And why is that?

Well, when you buy socks you'll often find a note that "one size fits all." Or there will be a vast recommended range of sizes, from 6 to 12, for instance. We're first amazed at the magical tendency for socks to fit widely different feet, but in actuality we're accommodating "bunching" in the heel or too much room in the toe, or too tight a sensation on the ankle. But, what can we do, "one size fits all."

Hence, the TV commercials promoting separate sizes in socks just as there are in—guess what—shoes! Imagine a shoe where "one size fits all." You'd have some ruined feet, no accomplished dancing whatsoever, and probably a lot of health problems and lawsuits.

We're engaged in a society where we are pressured to be like everyone else every day. Normative pressure is huge. The herd mentality is abundant and perverse.

Creating meaning and fulfilling a legacy are not about blanket approaches or common endeavors, similar dreams or conformism. Legacy is as individualized as a golfer's swing, a car's handling, or a contralto's voice.*

The superficiality of size refers to "bigger" not necessarily being better, and that size has to be appropriate to the person and the pursuit. Large size doesn't help a spelunker or a jockey. High speed doesn't mean much for a brain surgeon or watch maker.

What does this mean for us? How do we intelligently conduct our lives and our creation of legacy unless we change the metrics for our success? Herewith are some suggestions for disregarding metrics and standards and comparisons that don't help us, but rather force us into the herd.

This is the fallacy of "searching for meaning" as if it's Noah's Ark or a pot of gold at the end of a metaphysical rainbow.

Legacy is about creating meaning. There is no guru on the mountaintop. People trekking up the iconic Mt. Everest have turned it into a dump of human waste, detritus of climbing gear, and the general litter of humans in herds. Recently, people were lined up for hours to get to the summit, as though it were a Disney ride but no one had an express pass. *And during these final ascents, the amateur climbers walk over frozen, encased bodies of prior, amateur climbers, embedded in the ice.*

---

* Although I will admit I could not tell the difference between Margaret Whiting and Wayne Newton singing the same song unless I was looking at them.

That wonderfully sums up the "search" for meaning: we trample bodies of those before us, leaving a wake of waste, for a brief view which is threatening our own existence as we seek it.*

If "one size does not fit all" then what are we to do?

We need to examine our lives and value and intentions. We need to create meaning that represents our "calling" at the moment (remember the cathedral and bringing people closer to God) and can change as we grow, mature, and learn.

Meaning is fungible. It can and should change as we experience life. The question becomes one of whether we're experiencing life and do we fully understand the experience?

For now, ask yourself these questions:

- What are the values that guide my life daily? Are they conscious so that I can deliberately act on them, and make decisions within that context?
- What contributions do I make to those around me regularly? Am I sharing and generous or withholding and selfish? This isn't solely about money. It's about time, ideas, support, and resources.
- Do I make a difference? Do others listen and heed what I say, do they gain from my actions, are they pleased that I'm present? Have I persuaded people in terms of their best interests and not merely my own? Have I sacrificed when needed to help others?
- Do I change my values as I learn and grow? Do I contribute toward understanding and rationality rather than polarization? Am I able to accommodate changing times and requirements?

---

* In these lines it is not uncommon for people to die of exposure, oxygen deprivation, and underlying, prior medical conditions. They are simply passed by those behind them.

- How will people remember me? Will they talk about my accomplishments, my wealth, my credentials? Or will they talk about who I was and how I contributed to their own well-being and growth? Will I have been a role model for values and positive behaviors?

You may find these questions difficult to answer, but the real problem is that they're difficult to ask. One size doesn't fit all. Ask yourself what size fits you. Your value, your legacy, are bespoke, not "off the rack."

CHAPTER 4

Smarts, As We Say in New York

Legacy is amazingly pragmatic and "in the trenches." Street smarts aren't taught, they're learned, but not all over, and they provide proportion. David wouldn't win every time once the slingshot trick was apparent, and Voltaire observed that "God is on the side of the heaviest battalions." The amount and size of your prayers don't make you more likely to reach heaven. Luther simply wanted a hearing but the Pope wanted to make an example of him and he inadvertently changed the world. Once you're an "underdog" in people's perceptions, you're no longer an underdog in reality.

The Over/Under on David and Goliath

Our culture (and I mean global culture) is rife with the "common person" uprooting and toppling the larger-than-life. Socially, the "life of the party" can be a minor bureaucrat at work. In sports we love to see the emergence of a Muhammad Ali or a tennis 16-year-old wunderkind. In business we cherish the likes of a Steve Job and the fact that Bill Hewlett and Dave Packard started HP in their garage. We're emotionally involved when a small country's athletes can win the gold at the Olympics. How many stories about entertainment involve someone in the chorus getting a break and emerging as a "star," as in *A Star Is Born*?

So we may come to believe that our legacy is based on the luck of the draw. Both of my kids are in the entertainment business, and I'm astounded at the degree of luck influencing who is chosen and on what basis, an ongoing roulette wheel. Talent doesn't always "out." Even as a writer—and I have over 60 books in 15 languages to my credit—I've found that an agent or acquisitions editor may accept or reject a manuscript for reasons that have nothing to do with its quality. There could have been an argument with a spouse, a compliment from the boss, or a loss on the Giants' game the prior day. It could be before or after lunch that makes the difference.

However, your legacy is not about the "luck of the draw" or happenstance. You *do* create and control it. Even theologically we may cite David and Goliath, but once the Philistines saw the slingshot trick they wouldn't have fallen for that again. Goliath would have won two out of three.

My father enlisted in the paratroops when they were first formed prior to Pearl Harbor. He was sent for training in the South, to Ft. Benning in Georgia. There was a great deal of prejudice at the time. My father took up boxing, defeated 11 opponents, and retired undefeated. His sergeant said, "Weiss, you're one smart Jew." When I asked him why he retired he told me, "I knew the next guy who would be in line and I knew I couldn't beat him."

We all hear of people who stayed too long in their fields, who couldn't surrender the limelight. I think Sinatra was the greatest popular singer of all time, the greatest interpreter of the Great American Songbook, as it's called. But near the end of his career when his health became the obstacle, his voice was mostly gone, and he was reading his lyrics from teleprompters. (I know this because I spoke from a stage the day before he was to sing at The Golden Nugget and they had installed a series of teleprompter screens flush with the stage.)*

Many athletes hang on too long because they don't want to leave the accolades and the adulation. But they then detract from their legacy.

---

* My colleague, Dan Gilbert at Harvard, tells me that Sinatra never thought he was no longer on top of his game, and most people at that level don't. We respectfully disagree.

Muhammad Ali did that, as well. As I write this, the question in professional football is whether Tom Brady has hung on too long, even departing his team of 20 years to remain active. (Reading this now, you'll have the answer.)

What do we do about the "David and Goliath" effect of the "one-time" place of glory, or the seeming luck involved at so many junctures in life, or the mundanity of our lives?

We have to practice "smarts":

Identify Why You Are Successful Where You Are Successful

We tend to focus on failures, not successes. Yet, the easiest way to identify and perpetuate our "smarts" is by replicating success. The entire focus on such ideas as "10,000 hours of practice" is predicated on the fact that the more you do something well the better you are in less time in the future. Although the Philistines would presumably be wise to David in the future, he knew how to use the slingshot from past practice. His victory wasn't an accident or a "lucky shot."

Remember That Simple Trumps Complex

We feel we have to construct elaborate solutions to problems and that the more complicated they are the more impressive and valuable they are. But all you usually achieve is a modern Rube Goldberg machine.* Occam's razor states that the shortest and easiest answer is also usually the best. I've told countless clients that, if something hurts, stop doing it and substitute something else. The briefest solutions are the most elegant solutions.

---

* Rube Goldberg was a popular cartoonist of the mid-20th century who devised elaborate machinery for simple tasks, such as pouring orange juice or swatting a fly. I provide this for those of you too young to have experienced his great work.

Blow Your Own Horn

We hear a great deal of moralizing about orchestras that require a leader to play together well, but small bands and string quartets seem to do quite well on their own. And even in the large orchestra, everyone in the brass section is blowing their own horn. Your smarts have to be on "display." Legacies, by definition, can't be "hidden" or undiscovered. Don't be afraid through false modesty or humility to let people know you have an answer or an idea.

Talk the Walk

We hear all the time about "walking the talk," meaning that we should practice what we preach. Fair enough. But the reciprocal is to "talk the walk," meaning you have to let people know what you're doing, who you are, what you're capable of accomplishing. Behaviors are fine, but not everyone sees you all the time. You don't have to merely have good ideas and contribute; you have to document your experiences and results.

The creation of meaning in your life has to be manifest, has to be expressed in order to make a difference in the world, to create a legacy. This isn't an intellectual pursuit, but rather a visceral one. You have to feel it, and you have to allow others to see your actions as a result.

David didn't have to do a risk analysis, or receive a vote of confidence from the troops, or consult about the latest slingshot technology. He knew why he was there and what had to be done.

There Is No Such Thing as an "Underdog"

The "underdog" is a person who is considered to have very little chance of winning a competition. We tend to root for the underdog, because he or she evokes pity or even empathy. We have an emotional attachment. Sometimes the underdog prevails, such as the "miracle on ice" of 1980 when an amateur US hockey team defeated a professional Soviet team *en route* to the Olympic gold medal. Sometimes the underdog is simply a person who evokes great empathy although there is zero chance of victory, such as Britain's Eddie the Eagle, the ski jumper who managed to qualify for the Olympics despite his very pitiful abilities. He finished dead last, but they've written books and made movies about him. (And he did hold the British ski jump record. Apparently, the Brits aren't thrilled about hurtling down a hill and leaping into the air at 60 miles per hour.)

However, we often root for the underdog because we identify with the underdog. We feel life has passed us by, or given us a lousy route, or delivered some pretty bad luck. Someone else—the fates, our siblings, our friends, our enemies, our boss, the government, lawyers—has controlled our destiny, written our biographies, denied us our legacy.

We don't like to admit this, most of the time, although victimization has become the rallying point for some social and political leaders. People *are* victimized at times, certainly some people more so than others by ethnicity, color, gender, disability, and so forth.

But you can be victimized without being a victim. We can focus on real and perceived injustices and unfair competition, or we can focus on our own abilities and talents and control. In most cases for most people, we have more control than we think we do. The fact is, *we tend to surrender our control, which is why we think we have very little control.* We give it away.

People often don't vote, either because they think it doesn't matter, or they are complacent (or can't be bothered to go to the polls). We don't complain, accepting shoddy goods and rude service. We tend to "make do" instead of "make it again." You can see what I'm talking about in the graphic in Figure 4.1.

If we feel all control is external, driven by others or the fates, we endure a Calvinistic kind of predestination where it's senseless to try to change. People who reject medical treatment might say, "It's in God's hands." The opposite is the land of the motivational speaker, who will tell you that you're your own best friend and can do anything you like, it's *all* in your control.

In fact, control is reciprocal, a blend of the world impacting us (taxes, disease, rules, weather) and our impacting the world (tax shelters, vaccinations,

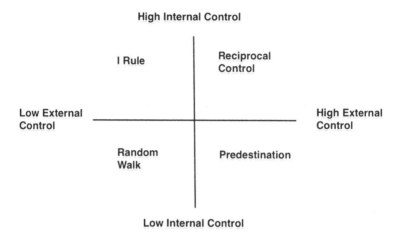

Figure 4.1 *Sources of control.*

exceptions to the rules, moving the party indoors). If we view these relationships intelligently, *we are never the underdog unless we allow ourselves to be.* No one can intimidate (or motivate) you. You decide to allow intimidation or to create motivation.

Here are some specifics on avoiding the underdog mentality and instead being a dog "in the hunt":

Don't Fall for the "Humility Hype"

There are people who claim that "humility" is a key element for success. Yet I've never seen huge amounts of humility flowing from Warren Buffet, or a hospital chief of surgery, or Venus and Serena Williams, or Alan Dershowitz, or Tiger Woods. The people chanting about the virtues of humility are, indeed, themselves humble, *because they have no great accomplishments.* Here's what humility really is, because it's not about degrading your own achievements: *humility is about the realization and behavior that others have worth and talent and should be respected.* Do you really want a humble heart surgeon, or one who believes he or she is God in the operating room?

Mindset Often Trumps Physical Attributes

I don't play golf, it's too much like work. But I do enjoy watching the championship matches because they reveal more about the mentality of the players and their management of the course and their emotions than they do about physical attributes. Seldom does the player with the longest drive win the game. Golfers at the highest level are attacked by nerves and make amateur shots and bad errors. Their putting, which requires fine motor skills, can deteriorate to an embarrassing level of inaccuracy.* It's the way you "manage" the situation and control your emotions that allows you to win. Don't "blow up" when you're confronted, simply smile and assume the expert's role. Don't miss the putt because you're nervous.

Don't Give up the Ship

When asked to surrender, John Paul Jones said, "I have not yet begun to fight!" and defeated a British ship much larger than his own, which was sinking under him. He had to transfer his crew to the defeated ship. Tom Brady and the Patriots came from 25 points down in the third quarter to defeat the Atlanta Falcons in the Super Bowl when they had about a two percent chance of winning at that point. The players interviewed after the game said, "We never gave up and just did our individual jobs." *Most people don't actually lose, they give up.*

Of course, you don't want to go through life as the underdog, as the person no one expects to win. That's no legacy. The legacy of the Patriots at this writing is six Super Bowl wins. The legacy of John Paul Jones is that of a great fighting captain.

Why Voltaire Had It Right

When everyone was fighting in the name of God and was convinced God was on their side in the 18th century, the wit and satirist Voltaire pointed out that "God is on the side of the heaviest battalions which shoot the best."

---

* In the Masters Tournament in 1996, one of the great golfers of all time, Greg Norman, blew a six-shot lead on the final day and lost the tournament by five strokes.

Damon Runyon, the legendary reporter who covered Broadway and whose work was the origin for *Guys and Dolls*, said, "The race isn't always to the fastest nor the battle to the strongest, but that's the way to bet."

In other words, Goliath would win two out of three.

One of the aspects of understanding and utilizing control discussed earlier is that it creates power. Power isn't always hierarchical or due to wealth. Power is often based on expertise, courage, and respect. Some call this "informal power," I call it "referent power," meaning we refer to (and defer to) people who have charisma, charm, accomplishment, and confidence.

So to emulate those "heavy battalions that shoot well" we have to possess power. Have you ever walked into a room and simply sensed someone had the respect and deference of others? What is power derived from, and how does it relate to our "story"?

- Language: We need to have a command of our language, a wide vocabulary, and the ability to use metaphors, similes, examples, and other figures of speech. The pathetic notion espoused by some that we should "dumb down" our language and not try to feel superior to others originates with people who don't have command of the language and don't want to try to gain it. So they seek to bring others down to their level.

Write down any word you encounter that you don't know and look it up when you can. Then use it for the next week frequently, and you'll have command of it.

- Confidence: Our self-esteem can't be as high as our last victory or as low as our last defeat. It has to be constant and positive. Efficacy is how well you can do something, but self-worth means that you're valuable whether or not you do something well. You aren't a "failure" if you fail to get a piece of business, have an argument with your kids, or buy a poor stock.

Identify your good acts and your victories. Keep reminding yourself that you may have setbacks but that you're still a good and decent person. If you can forgive others, you can certainly forgive yourself.

- Resilience: We all suffer setbacks but some of us remain "down" while others bounce back. "Resilience" is the ability to recover quickly and to return to a positive mentality.

Don't wallow in self-pity and self-doubt when something goes wrong. Most of all, don't feel guilty. Find the cause of the problem and remove it. If you must, apologize or start again. But don't keep fretting. A pothole in the road can be annoying, even jarring, but you don't stop driving because of it.

- Critical thinking skills: You need to separate out intellect and emotion. The former urges us to think and the latter to act. Too many of us immediately act emotionally and later regret what we said or did, often with a comment or behavior that's hard to retract or take back. Think before you act unless you're running from a bear or escaping a fire, neither of which is very likely.

Take a few minutes and ask yourself what is the problem to be solved? What is the decision to be made? What is the plan to implement? What is the opportunity to be exploited? Once you've made a rational decision, by all means act with courage and speed. But get identification and action in the right order.

If we combine these, it might look like Figure 4.2.

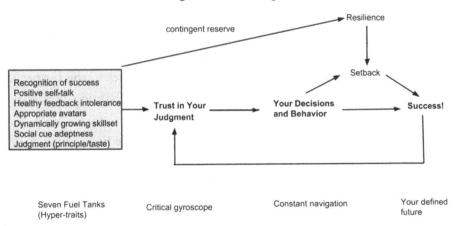

Figure 4.2   *Resilience and critical thinking.*

The seven traits on the left "fuel" resilience and create trust in your own judgment (the thinking before the acting). When your decision might be wrong, they serve as the contingency to get you back on track.

The "heaviest battalions" are, metaphorically, created by people who have the right tools, the right attitudes, and the right commitment. They don't fear being wrong, they don't dwell on guilt, they don't try "not to lose." They strive to win. Guilt, fear, and stress "mask" talent. No one operates at his or her best when burdened with these emotions. No one can "shoot straight."

The "heaviest battalions" as far as we're concerned are about having the skills, talents, energy, and confidence to move forward, overcome setbacks, and exploit successes. Archimedes said, "Give me a lever and I can move the world."

Here's another example.

How Luther Changed the World

Martin Luther was ordained a priest in 1507. He was a professor of theology in Germany. He was appalled by many Catholic practices, most especially indulgences, which could be bought to ensure one's entry into heaven in the afterlife. People tolerated corrupt clergy, including cardinals with children and mistresses, because life was short and hard and these indulgences would provide a means to live eternally in nirvana.

Pope Leo X refused to meet with him as did Charles V, the Emperor. Luther threatened the legitimacy of the papacy by claiming that entry into heaven was solely dependent on good works and that the Bible, not the Pope, was the final authority on theology. Because he couldn't make a case in front of those in power—he was excommunicated—he actually fractured the then-Christian world and created the Protestant Reformation. He translated the Bible into the German vernacular, making it accessible to those who couldn't read it before. But that's not what he had set out to do!

Luther was not all that different from the corrupt clergy in that he went on to advocate violent views toward Jews, Roman Catholics, Anabaptists, and others.

Luther changed the world. He was justifiably upset with the corruption of the Catholic Church, and felt that reforms were needed. In all likelihood, if the Pope had agreed to meet with him and accept some of the reforms quite clearly required, that would have been the end of it. Instead, the Christian world was permanently in schism.

"Smarts" can change the world. Luther didn't set out to create the Reformation. He was a monk and a professor. But he was outraged at corruption. Today, we have "whistle blowers" in business and government. (I advised one personally who saw illegal and unethical conduct in a major drug company, and he collected about $25 million as the "reward.") But do we need to pay people who see a better way, who are fed up with lying and incompetence, who seek redress of grievances?

No one is quite sure if Luther tacked his opposition to a church door, but he did make it known to the general population in Europe *without benefit of an internet or mass communications.* What does this mean for us?

In a world constantly trying to "homogenize" us, we need to step out of the herd. Our legacy has to be not one of conformance or comfort but of confrontation and commitment. Jesus "comforted the afflicted and afflicted the comfortable."

Colin Kaepernick started a huge movement when he, alone, knelt during the national anthem prior to a football game. Tarana Burke began the "me too" movement in 2006. Now Harvey Weinstein, one of the wealthiest, most powerful men in entertainment, is in jail and famous news people like Matt Lauer and Charlie Rose have lost their jobs in disgrace. Positively, Steve Jobs launched Apple, Fred Smith launched FedEx, Jeff Bezos began Amazon, and Elon Musk, Tesla.

---

* What little we know about Jesus is from the massive writings of St. Paul, whom many regard as the original "viral marketer," moving from place to place and urging others to relay his message from place to place.

It only takes one person to begin a movement, to propel their calling, to force others to think and change their views. Luther didn't try to create a cohort of priests or take surveys. He simply pointed out the inequities in the system and let people decide for themselves. He died excommunicated, but his actions have affected history. It merely takes one person, and whether that one person changes the world, or the country, or the neighborhood, or the family—or just you—it is significant. Think about your earlier life. Was there a person or were there people who made a profound difference? It could have been a coach, or a teacher, or a distant relative, or a friend. It could have been someone who made you responsible and accountable, or someone who gave you a break.

Here is my social proof:

- Mrs. Grothheusen
- Mrs. Stephanour
- Mrs. Fleming
- Miss Mandelkern
- Mrs. Bowman
- Mrs. O'Brien
- Miss Baratini
- Mrs. Johnson
- Mrs. Lippert
- Mr. Heitman

Can you guess who they are? The answer is in the footnote below.*

We can all cite Mother Theresa, or Gandhi, or Martin Luther King, or even Fred Smith or Jeff Bezos, who served as models and inspirations for us. But the truth is that such inspiration is usually from more intimate

---

* My grammar school teachers, from Kindergarten through 8th grade in Union City, New Jersey. It was a converted cheese factory in the inner city. But these wonderful people provided a great education, more important than my high school education. I feel like I'm in debt to all of them. I don't recall too many of my high school or university teachers and professors.

relationships. Unfortunately, we don't always recognize this huge asset at the time, but only when they are "gone."

And, more importantly, are you considering whether your legacy includes helping others in some similar fashion?

One question I ask all coaching clients who are undecided about whether to take action is, "If not now, when?"

CHAPTER 5

The Over-Magnification of Media

Bigger, faster, better: They carefully measure with chains for a first down in football after the ball is arbitrarily placed where an official's foot marks the forward progress! Does a hundredth of a second victory in a swim or footrace really indicate superiority? Just whose legacy are we talking about? The mediocre thrive on arbitrary assessments of merit and we succumb to it, from Nathan's Hot Dog Eating Contest to *America's Got Talent* (apparently, not on every show).

Why Is a Sub-Two-Hour Marathon an Accomplishment?

The first Olympic marathon race in 1896 (26.2 miles) was won in just short of three hours. If one could walk at a steady, healthy pace for three hours the distance covered would be about 9 miles. The record as I write this, about a century and a quarter later, is 2 hours. That amount of walking would only get you six miles away from your start. Increasing by a third in 25 years, if consistent, would mean that in 2050 the marathon record would be about 1.1 hours.

Is that possible?

Is it important?

The record for the mile run at this writing is 3:43 minutes. Roger Bannister broke the "four-minute mile" in 1954 at half a second below four minutes. That has been reduced by about 6 percent, meaning that 70 years from now the record might be 3.2.

Running the marathon and completing it are impressive, but not at the cost of losing your bodily functions or endangering your organs or dropping dead. Training for years to shave a second off the mile record makes no sense to me in terms of what one could be contributing to society.

Faster (or bigger or louder or taller) isn't always better. The steam locomotive Empire State Express made it from Albany to Manhattan in seven hours in 1890 regularly. Today, early a century and a half later, Amtrak can get you there … in eight hours, if you're lucky.

Sometimes metrics become meaningless. No one would argue that we want to increase the speed of EMTs reaching patients in crisis, or rescue attempts in natural disasters. But those aren't competitive sports, they're vital human needs.

In Dubai, which is Disneyland for adults with a lot of disposable income, they specialize in the only six-star hotel (Burj Al Arab), the tallest building (Burj Khalifa), highest restaurant (At.mosphere), and so on, *ad nauseum*. They have built two Chrysler Building replicas, a Leaning Tower of Pisa (with more of a lean), and on and on and on.

It quickly grows boring, particularly when the guide says, "We have more construction cranes than anywhere else on earth!"

In terms of meaning and legacy, *what is really an accomplishment?* Lindbergh proving that planes could fly the Atlantic and ushering in a new era of transportation might merit it. But can you tell me who holds the current world air speed record, or distance record, or altitude record at the moment? Don't bother waiting for it, I don't know and I'm not looking it up.

What should be the metrics of our accomplishments then?

An improved condition: We should create improvement in others, in the environment, in processes. We all improve incrementally, not normally in huge leaps. If you improve by just 1 percent a day, for example, in 70 days you'll be twice as good.* Here's Ralph Waldo Emerson:

To find the best in others, to give one's self, to leave the world a bit better, whether by a healthy child, a garden patch or a redeemed

---

* If you don't believe me, do the math on your calculator; keep multiplying 1 times 1 percent and you'll arrive, in 70 repeats, at 2.

social condition; to have played and laughed with enthusiasm and sung with exultation; to know even one life has breathed easier because you have lived—this is to have succeeded.

Generosity: The most impressive leaders I have ever met or observed are generous. They share information, resources, credit, and ideas. They aren't worried about being "ripped off," and they see their role as building abilities in others. I'm not talking about writing a check, I'm talking about building support.

Consistency: We've come to a point where a "fad" of a month is actually long-lived. Out metrics have to include longevity and reliability. It's quite appropriate for someone to change his or her belief system. But it's not appropriate to do that to gain favor with an "in crowd" or be popular at parties. When I've surveyed people about their most important traits in a leader, "consistency" has been a primary factor, so that people know what to expect. Avoiding hypocrisy and our parents' admonitions to "do as I say not as I do," as if their role modeling didn't matter, are absurd. I've never known how someone can adamantly oppose abortion, for example, yet support capital punishment or vice versa.

Passion: I watched from the back of the room as a low-key executive somberly droned on about a very positive year and full bonus pots. Someone next to me from the company asked, "Are we being fired?" When I role-play with my coaching clients I find their greatest lack isn't content or expertise but rather *passion*. They don't convince others because they are strictly logical and rational, which may make people think, but not emotional, which makes people act!

An improved condition, generosity, consistency, and passion. How do you measure up? Where can you improve? Running the marathon in 2 hours 2 minutes, or 1 hour 58 minutes (or 4 hours and 9 minutes) doesn't matter. What matters is what you leave behind of substance for others to appreciate and to benefit from.

A Hundredth of a Second Is Ridiculous

A hundredth of a second is ten milliseconds. A normal blink of your eye takes about 100 milliseconds—ten times as long. Do I have your attention?

We arbitrarily reduce accomplishment to technological minutiae. We once had a "photo finish" in horse races, based on the latest technology of the times, where the stewards would try to determine which horse's nose first crossed the finish line. Even the fastest camera, or its angle, could undermine this pseudo-scientific pursuit. My favorite millisecond measure today is in competitive swimming, where a touch-pad records whose fingertip first touched the pool side after 100 meters (or thousands of meters) of fanatic swimming.

Is that about the best swimmer, or the longest swimmer, or the most finger dexterity, or slight imperfections in the responsiveness of the equipment?

Is one tennis player better than another when the match point depends on a ball hitting the net and bouncing on one side or the other, no skill involved whatsoever, except having lasted that long? What about the lucky basketball shot from half-court to win a championship, or the subjective judging of a figure skating routine? (The French judge has awarded a 9.7 and the Romanian judge a 6.8. Are they watching the same routine, or is one of the other competitors Romanian? Or has the judge's breakfast caused some digestive distress?)

We have forgotten truly outstanding people who were overshadowed by someone by a hundredth of a second or a fraction of an inch. There have been fantastic movies, plays, speeches, contributions of all sorts that have been lost in the noise from some record being broken or some personality being hoisted as the new poster person. (Michael Phelps, the much bemedaled Olympic swimmer, has always seemed that way to me.)

When I was in Manila, I visited clubs with better American music than I've heard in America, finer singers and superior musicians. Here at home I've heard little-known regional groups that were great, and I've seen productions on Broadway that make you scratch your head wondering who on earth invested in such poor talent. After all, I do have some swampland in Florida that I'd be willing to part with for the right price.

We can't allow ourselves and our legacy to be evaluated by such flawed standards. That's why meaning is self-created. What's created *around us* is often inapplicable or plain wrong. Hot-dog eating contests are novelties (and rather disgusting) but the athletic competitor who brags about hurting others and driving them out of the game is malicious (and disgusting).

John Havlicek is a Hall of Fame basketball player whose career with the Boston Celtics was originally as the "sixth man." He would enter the game when needed—he wasn't a starter—and his presence often then made the difference. He was fine with that role and became one of the greatest players in the history of the game. He's probably most remembered for stealing the ball from the Philadelphia 76ers in 1965 at the last minute to preserve a championship. He was never the fastest or the tallest or the highest point producer.

He was simply great in the role.

We need to lay waste to the claims that a millisecond determines "best." I mean that metaphorically. While I'd never endorse "participation awards" because I believe in the recognition of talent and excellence, I will tell you that perfectionism kills excellence. One can be excellent, *along with colleagues*, alone, or in a crowd. But perfectionism will leave everyone frustrated and unsuccessful.

The meaning in life we pursue should not be about being "perfect" by anyone's standards. The media tend to over-accentuate this, highlighting "perfect 10s" in competitions and a "perfect business strategy" or performance. You don't experience perfection in life: not in a medical procedure, an airplane flight, or a dinner. They may be terrific, even unprecedented (if you don't get out much), but they're not perfect.

The search for meaning in perfection causes massive procrastination from people who aren't ready to let go until they have everything perfect. *They prefer the critique of being late rather than risk the critique that what they've produced isn't "perfect."*

The fallacy of the hundredth of a second, when extrapolated, becomes the fallacy of "the final 20 percent." My contention is that when you're 80 percent ready, you move.

When you try to add the final 20 percent to a speech, the audience doesn't appreciate the difference; to a book, the reader doesn't appreciate the difference; to a discussion, the participants don't appreciate the difference.

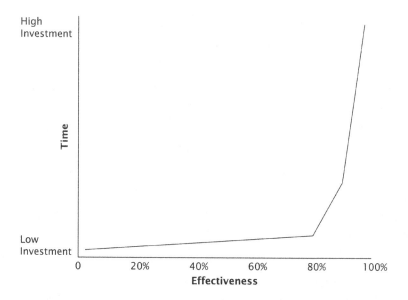

Figure 5.1   *Eighty percent ready.*

Figure 5.1 shows the "hockey stick" increase in labor to achieve an ephemeral final 20 percent.

Perfectionism is the search for the final 20 percent, that final millisecond, that really makes no difference to the meaning of your life. Think of all those people eternally disappointed because they "lost" by a fraction of an inch or a hundredth of a second.

On second thought, don't.

The Official's Foot

I've been nearly giddy with the faith we put in the imperfect. People tell me they're "not people of faith." Well, how is it you drive two car lengths behind the car in front of you at 75 MPH with the car behind you even closer?* We have faith in the mechanics who have worked on our plane, and the

---

* The late, great comedian George Carlin pointed out that the driver in front of you going so slow is a moron and the driver tailgating so closely is an idiot.

cleanliness of the kitchen in the restaurant preparing our food. (One of the social justice issues, of course, is that people of color and others can't have the same amount of faith that many of us do in the judicial, health, educational, or legal systems, to name a few such areas, and with good reason.)

The tired cliché about when you "assume" it makes an "ass" out of "u" and "me" ought to be buried somewhere. I assume the other driver will observe the red light and that my doctor knows the drug side effects, and that there will not be another comet hitting the Yucatan again tomorrow.

However, small things elude us or we allow ourselves to be duped. American football, which is resplendent with replays, superimposed first-down markers, and coaching via the quarterback's helmet earpieces, relies on the foot of an official to mark the spot of forward motion of a ball.

Thus: the official sees what is believed to be the most forward spot, then has to equalize that with a spot below, on the turf, and then marks the spot with a foot, since the ball isn't immediately available. Officials, of course, have different size feet, and some use their left foot, some their right. Then the new ball is placed beside their foot. I think you can plainly "see" that there is plenty of room for an error of inches, easily.

Yet, for the first down measurement, the officials meticulously and officiously bring in chains attached to rods carefully calibrated to exactly measure ten yards (the distance needed for a first down) and apply this very strict marker to all the variations resulting from the official's foot. And the first down is often made or missed by an inch or less, far smaller than the variation (margin of error) allowed for in the convoluted mechanical process described above.

Games and championships have been won or lost on the measurement of such a first down late in the game. We have faith in the integrity of the game, of the objectivity of the officials, and of the players and coaches who will honor these outcomes. *And we extend that faith preposterously to the official's foot placement.*

Does this explain why a government that can maintain roads *also* receives our trust about waging war or fighting illnesses? Does it explain why a valued role-model whose advice has been helpful can so easily con us out of our life savings? Does it explain why we believe others are in a position to tell us what meaning is, what our legacy should be, and how to think and act?

All too often, I believe it does. This is exacerbated by the same media which focus on the football, the official's foot, the replay, and the actual outcome *with far more of an interest in exposing mistakes than in confirming accuracy.*

The media over-represent "expertise" because the media are focused on sensation and not the mundane. Most storm warnings are absurdly over-rated, and most political commentary is absurdly biased. The sports commentators keep talking about "it's all of matter of where they spot the ball" as if that's the telling mark. Yet that mark is subjective, as explained above. If tennis can have automation that determines if a ball is on the line or over the line, why can't a football carry a chip that places it at a very precise point on the field?

Why does the choreography of the "scientific" measurement of the chains first rely on the subjective determination of the official's foot? That's like improvising a ballet. It doesn't work very well.

The point here is that there are hundreds of points in any athletic competition where the game is being decided, bit by bit. We and the media tend to focus on the last play of the game, the key error, the unlikely shot, the last-minute score. But why should we blame the person who made an error at the end of the game to lose it when much earlier in the game six batters failed to deliver a hit to score the runners who were on base? Who's more at fault?

When I hear a newsreader use the illiterate "between you and I" phrase, I also wonder how the news writer made the error, the teleprompter writer didn't catch the gaffe, as well as how the on-camera talent can mindlessly repeat it. A typo in this book you're reading—and you'll probably find one or two—means that I might have made the error, the proofreader didn't see it, and the final readers of the book's proofs missed it.*

---

* There are obsessive/compulsive typo-finders out there. When one comes to me and proudly proclaims four typos have been found, expecting me to do something about it, I reply, "There are actually seven typos, you'd better go back." Fair warning.

"Meaning" derives from real issues of significant importance and not trivialities. We can't invest too much meaning in a hundredth of a second of the official's foot, and we can't invest too little in our contributions and support. We can't rely on the media or other sources to dictate what's important and meaningful.

That's up to us. Being "first" isn't as important as being meaningful.

The "First" Nonsense

If we can't be the absolute first, we can be the "identify first." By that I mean we tend to divide "firstness" by:

- Gender
- Ethnicity
- Language
- "Ableness"
- Geography
- Frequency
- Duration
- Equipment
- Distance
- Education

We are fixated on the "first" by identify and category, which may strongly influence our search for meaning.

Rhode Island Monthly Magazine has a very clever contest each year where readers (and others) vote for "best of." But the categories are more numerous than the inhabitants of an ant colony. You can have "best latte in south county" or "finest New York Wiener system in Providence" or "best long distance running shoe under $25" (I exaggerate only slightly—I think there are at least two-dozen categories for best doctor). The result is that everyone can win, it's like a participation prize, and the magazine sells ads to the contenders and hosts a party for everyone when the results are in.

I think this is brilliant on the part of the publication because it trades on the need for everyone to be first in something, no matter if the plethora of qualifiers create a very narrow field—sometimes of one!* But in a world where "identity" has tended to trump talent, we see peculiar results.

Why is there still a "Best Actor" category at the Academy Awards or Golden Globes for men and for women, separately? Why not simply "best actor"? In an age of gender fluidity, why make the distinction? Why is dressage or chess or pool (billiards) separated by gender? If physical attributes aren't a requirement, then why discriminate?

Louis Brandeis became the first Jewish Supreme Court justice, Thurgood Marshall the first African-American, Sandra Day O'Connor the first female, and Antonin Scalia the first Italian-American. These appointments occurred between 1916 and 1986. We've tended to see "seats" reserved ever since for people with these backgrounds.

Choose the identify in addition to those mentioned—indigenous people, combinations of ethnicity foreign born, LGBTQ, and so forth—and we have a multitude of "firsts" which relate more to background than accomplishment. It's not that these individuals aren't talented, it's that they (and, seemingly, the rest of us) are engaged in symbolic "firsts." Moreover, this often has a negative influence.

Jeremy Boorda was the Chief of Naval Operations in the US, the highest rank in the service. *He was the first American sailor to have risen through the enlisted ranks to that exalted position.* In other words, he did not attend the US Naval Academy.

He was criticized at one point for wearing a combat ribbon that it was claimed he hadn't earned.† There was an unprecedented controversy in the service. When he learned a magazine article was about to be published about the "scandal," he killed himself.

---

* When government agencies send out requests for proposals (RFPs) they are sometimes so unique in their requirements (e.g., must speak Spanish and French, has published two books on the topic, has proprietary assessment tools) that there is only one qualifier, even though it's technically "competitive bidding."

† These are the rows of tiny ribbons arrayed on one's dress uniform, often totally 30 or more.

His "first" was outside the norms, and he was not accorded the benefit of the doubt that others would have received who had graduated from Annapolis. (This is similar to "white privilege" claims today.) Apparently, he could not stand the shame when the system wouldn't support him.

I discussed Eddie the Eagle earlier who, although no world-class athlete, was the *first* to represent the UK in the Olympic ski jump. Gender, ethnicity, origins, education, *even novelty*, all count for firsts. So does the best cappuccino between first and ninth streets in a town of less than 10,000 citizens. When you extrapolate this what you do arrive at are participation awards, which undermine true talent and accomplishment.

Your meaning shouldn't be about "firsts" no matter how broad or narrow. It should focus on contribution, support, involvement, help, decency, and similar traits. For every Mother Teresa there are thousands of nuns laboring in remote places helping people through ordeals and misery. For every Ford Foundation there are people who give more than they can afford to assist a neighbor or someone down on their luck.

I leave you now with this quote from the writer Joseph Epstein: "*The true measure of generosity is not how much one gives but how much, after giving, one has left over.*"*

---

* From his book *A Line Out for A Walk*, W.W. Norton, 1992.

CHAPTER 6

The Challenge and Necessity
of Vulnerability

Counterintuitively, perhaps, legacy is about humility. As humans, we need to connect and interact. This requires vulnerability and reciprocity. It also requires honesty. We talk about "sportsmanship" and "how you play the game" amidst doping scandals and cheating. Even the lofty Olympics plays the national anthem only of the winner, who stands on a podium above others, and they maintain a national medal count during the games. Our competition and the *caste system it creates are the antithesis of connecting and communicating.*

We Can't Connect if We're Not Vulnerable

I happen to love lobster. I'm fascinated by these creatures, as well, because no one knows how long they live or how large they can grow. I've read about an 80-pound lobster being caught, and another that was thought to be a hundred years old.* Contrary to myth, large lobsters are not "tough" to eat. They need to be steamed, which is the best way to eat any lobster, because boiling or grilling removes a great deal of flavor. On Father's Day my wife traditionally treats me to a seven-pound lobster.

---

* Recently an 11-year-old raked up a giant clam that is called a "quahog" in Rhode Island. It turns out that a similar one found in cold, North Atlantic waters was at least 500 years old!

Lobsters have exoskeletons—a shell, as opposed to humans' internal skeleton. Thus, they have to shed their shell—molt—in order to grow and then form a larger one. During this time the lobster is vulnerable to predators since its main defensive weapon has disappeared. So the lobster seeks shelter until the new shell hardens. This can be repeated countless times, so unless a predator or disease befalls the lobster, it will simply keep growing. If a clam can live for over 500 years, why can't a lobster?

Thus, I've coined "the lobster principle," which holds that we can't grow without sufficient vulnerability. Think of the mastermind groups, the teams, and similar collections of people in which you've been involved. Some people give a lot of advice but never ask questions. Some people are mostly quiet. Some people solely boast of their "victories."

But the people who learn the most are those who share their defeats, uncertainties, and discomforts. They shed their defensive "shell." And unlike the crustacean, there is no enemy after us. *We create our "shells" to protect our egos, not our lives.* We don't have to hide from predators.

My lobster principle demands that we reveal our feelings and weaknesses to others in order to learn and to grow. We can't create meaning for ourselves if our lives are dedicated to protecting our repute, or our accolades, or our "perfection." I don't mind someone bragging about a hard-fought victory if they've also shared some humbling defeats. I call people who only show up when they want to boast "drive-by braggarts." I'm sure you can easily think of a few in your life.

Meaning is about contribution, fulfillment, and support. It's not about status, or ego needs, or winning.

Case Study: The Bank Executive

A bank executive whom I was hired to coach after he made a $16 million error after 20 years of unsurpassed achievement kept telling me he was fine, there was nothing wrong. He was highly resistant. And he looked pretty bad, very fatigued.

I asked if he was not sleeping well, if he had given up any of his hobbies, if he was increasingly irritable, if his relationship had changed with his wife in terms of intimacy, if his appetite had declined, and if he had less energy lately. Some of you know that this is a brief checklist for clinical depression.

He admitted to all of them, and I then asked if depression was to be found in his family, since it's often hereditary. He admitted to that, as well, and he told me he suspected he was seriously depressed but didn't want to tell anyone or seek help. He was afraid of being branded as "sick" and seen as a pariah.

I explained that he had an illness that was treatable, and we enrolled him in the company's employee assistance program. He engaged in therapy and took some medication, regained his former strength, and the following year showed a record profit for his division.

This was a 60-year-old man with a fabulous track record who was afraid of admitting to any kind of weakness, even after it had become apparent. His superiors thought the worst, which was that he had lost his skills, but at least they thought enough of him to invest in an outside coach to try to determine what the cause of his performance was.

How many people like this—many of whom you've known or are even related to—simply try to "tough it out" because they'd rather be in discomfort than be vulnerable?

You need to follow the example of the lobster if you seek a productive, long life. You have to learn by "molting":

- Create friends and groups with whom you can be completely honest and who won't judge you.
- Practice these dynamics yourself. Give people positive feedback instead of defaulting to negative critique.
- Assure others and assure yourself that "opening up" various aches and fears and guilt is helpful and productive.

- Build your ego positively. No matter whether you win or lose, succeed or fail in any given endeavor, it doesn't change your worth as a person contributing to others.

Don't allow your search for meaning to be a search for perfection or protection.

Why We Learn from Losing

The military academies study great defeats. It's as important to understand why a strategy or tactic *didn't* work as much as why others did work. The "impregnable" Maginot Line was easily circumvented by the Germans at the start of World War II. Hannibal was able to take elephants through "unsurpassable" mountains. Strong fortresses have been overcome by simply passing them by and isolating them.

Once we stop seeing "winning" and competing as such important elements for our egos and accept the necessity for vulnerability, we can begin to accept losing ("not winning" if that's too tough for you to utter). Someone gave me a tee-shirt that says, "Not everyone deserves a prize" in reaction to the insane "participation awards" that misinformed people try to bestow on every child. (A woman at a beach yelled at me, "You got that right!" when she read my shirt.)

Trying to obliterate or camouflage "losing" contributes to a huge loss of meaning. Schools have abandoned the "top ten" academic lists and ended valedictorian recognition and speeches. Everyone on every team gets a trophy for playing. Despite the fact we live in a highly competitive society—viz.: our addiction to sports and awards for entertainment and so forth—we're trying to tell our children it really doesn't matter. And this despite the fact that capitalism is all about talent and hard work in order to succeed.

So when we avoid even acknowledging losing (and "losers") we obliterate meaning. I'm not suggesting we become obsessed with our failures or dwell on our errors. I am suggesting that we can learn from examining our less than stellar performances:

- What we neglected to do which we knew we should have.
- What we didn't know which we should have.
- Why we were surprised and couldn't react properly.
- Why we couldn't stay calm and be resilient.

Making mistakes is how we learn.

Case Study: The Mistake

The general manager of a division of a large pharmaceutical company asked me to coach one of his direct reports who had just made a million-dollar error with a hospital client.

"Do you want me to help him find another job?" I asked.

"No, I want you to make sure he improves to the maximum using the million dollars we've just invested in his learning."

We've all met people who spend a great deal of their time covering up their mistakes. They blame others, they blame the environment, they blame the competition, they blame the government. They never accept blame, and they only become better, therefore, in dreaming up other sources to blame. They don't last all that long because we've all heard that song before.

Meaning is about improvement, not protection, growth and not defensiveness. I was conducting a workshop talking about innovation when a participant said, "I was with you about five or six years ago when you said exactly the opposite. You told me to do the reverse of what you just said!"

"I'm sure you're right," I said, "I found I was wrong back then and I've changed my approach."

He looked at me, speechless. Why shouldn't any of us be able to simply admit we're wrong about something? Of course, in a polarized society that becomes exceedingly difficult.

One of the greatest things I've learned from my losses is that it was my head, not my hands, that got in the way. I didn't hit the ball, didn't do well on the test, didn't get the date, because my nerves undermined my abilities. Once I realized that I had the means to overcome the cause of most of my failures. We tend to fear public speaking because we are afraid people will make fun of us, yet, pragmatically, no one attends a speech hoping that the speaker will fail and waste their time (except for the true sociopaths).

As you consider your legacy, consider both "wins" and "losses." If you watch a major professional golf championship, you'll find that the players are very similar in their talents but that they manage the course and their emotions in very different ways. I referred to Greg Norman earlier. In his book, *Second Wind*, legendary basketball star Bill Russell of the Celtics talks about the fact that true greatness is about playing at your absolute best when there is the absolute most pressure.[*]

You can learn to be bitter about losing, or blame the fates, or claim you were cheated, or withdraw from the competition in the future. But you can't withdraw from life. Meaning is reliant on knowing *why* you "win" and *why* you "lose" and maximizing the first while minimizing the second.

Once I learned the audience wanted me to succeed I became an excellent speaker, with no "nerves" impeding my performance. In many cases, we're our own worst enemies. We don't try things, we don't risk, we don't venture out. We're afraid of losing or being lost. But once you understand that losing is about learning and that no one can win them all, you're able to adapt a much calmer, pragmatic view of life.

That's the challenge of vulnerability: To face a loss and ask what you've learned. Whenever I've lost a proposal and failed to get the business, I've always asked the buyer, "What could I have done to have obtained your business?" I don't blame the buyers, I enlist them in my continuing improvement.

---

[*] Simon & Schuster, 1991.

Invention Is the Mother of Necessity

We need to create, to innovate, to invent. Necessity doesn't spawn invention from either parental side. Amazon, Apple, Uber, the original Sears Roebuck, the Wright brothers, Gutenberg, and FedEx were really not born of necessity. People were quite pleased. As Henry Ford observed, "If I had asked people what they wanted in terms of transportation, they would have told me, 'faster horses'."

I was happily living my life in 1985 when a woman called from out of the blue and we had this conversation:

"Is this Alan Weiss?"
"Yes."
"Do you own a Mercedes 450 SLC?"
"Yes." (I thought it was a recall.)
"How would you like to own one of the first car phones in New England?"
Brief pause: "How soon can you get here?"

I had not been moping around longing for a car phone (nor an automatic garage door opener 15 years earlier, nor a remote television channel changer). I don't recall being beside myself because the postal service couldn't guarantee a package delivery within one day.

The invention created the necessity.

This doesn't always work. Dean Kamen, with a history of brilliant innovations, created the Segway which went exactly nowhere (literally and figuratively). Fake crab turned out to be less than a food breakthrough. The jury is still out on driverless cars. Recreational drones have largely crash landed.

Our legacy is not reactive, but proactive. I know that sounds a bit odd, but it's nonetheless true. I'm not excluding our responding to need and conditions that need improvement. I'm simply suggesting that we are free to create need—to create necessity—with a better idea.

Too many times, people merely follow in the footsteps of those who came before. We're enhancing and augmenting others' legacies, perhaps, but hardly creating our own. Here's Matsuo Basho:

Don't follow in the footsteps of men of old. Seek what they sought.

There are three primary types of invention or innovation. (Famed Austrian economist Joseph Schumpeter called innovation "creative destruction.") They are:

Opportunism: We see something that "triggers" a creative idea on our part which we can immediately implement. When our town had a power outage early one morning, the local Dunkin' Donuts had to close. However, people who normally went there for coffee drove over anyway, believing it might be open. Instead, a man with a canteen truck—the kind that delivers coffee, pastries, and sandwiches to construction crews and worksites—pulled into the lot and sold out in about an hour. That driver was very opportunistic, figuring that people would be showing up at the coffee shop which was unable to open.

Conformist innovation: This is the ability to improve dramatically on an existing endeavor. The single-bullet rifle was replaced by a "repeating" rifle that held more shells. Solid tires were replaced by air-filled tires. Most recently and impressively, the taxi industry was disrupted by Uber, which is essentially a taxi service using advanced technology, cleaner cars, appointments, and so forth. The taxi industry which tried to block Uber no less than the Luddites attempted to block the creation of automated mills has now launched its own computer hailing and GPS services. It's not exactly rocket science to understand that customers don't want smelly, hot taxis driven by people who don't speak English, don't know the destinations, and keep talking on their cell phones.

Non-conformist innovation: This occurs when an entirely new way of operating is invented. Sears Roebuck grew because it used the new, transcontinental train system to send its catalogs all over the country, and accepted orders in the same way, then shipped the merchandise. Local general stores couldn't compete with the diversity and quality of Sears. More recently, Amazon has disrupted many industries by offering overnight delivery of a myriad of items and using complex algorithms to suggest products to patrons.

We didn't imagine we needed Uber or Amazon just as early settlers in the West were astounded by Sears.

Meaning isn't derived solely from what's around us. It can be generated from new approaches, new beliefs, changed values.

- What can you contribute that no one else can contribute in the same way that you can?
- What opportunities can you leverage to create your legacy?
- What relationships, or undertakings, or approaches that work well can you improve on still more?
- What can you create that no one else is providing?

These are questions we seldom ask ourselves or spend time considering. To answer them well, we need to connect with the world around us.

It Takes Courage to Connect

I've called "vulnerability" a challenge because it takes courage to lower your defenses and allow people to "touch" you emotionally and spiritually. (That's especially true these days when physical contact is considered rude and even dangerous!) My famous lobster has to hide to protect itself when vulnerable to predators.

But we're not talking about predators. We're talking about people we trust.

I was critiquing a book a woman was writing. She said, "You didn't exactly make my morning with your feedback," which was very direct and pretty tough. Before I could say anything she continued, "But that's why I like to work with you, you respect me enough to tell me the truth and not bend it to make me happy."

There's a term for that: tough love.

It takes courage to truly connect with others for feedback and learning because it can be very tough. We have to tuck our egos away and simply listen for the objective truth. That's not as difficult as you might think, not as painful as you might fear. Here's the question I recommend to everyone I counsel about relationships, whether a spouse, partner, sibling, parent, or child:

Was this act that is irritating or hurting you so much done deliberately to achieve that end?

Or is your irritation and hurt accidental or exaggerated, or fictitious? As upset as I used to get when I couldn't find the TV remote which my wife had used last, I came to realize that she didn't deliberately hide it to make me suffer. She probably took a phone call and happened to have it in her hand. As much as I can be irritated with the oblivious person chatting with the bank teller about grandchildren while a serpentine line waits to get near the counter, that person hasn't decided to punish any of us in line.

Being self-absorbed, or being unself-aware, as annoying as it may be, is seldom done with the intent of discomfiting others. It's simply an oblivious act which happens to discomfit others.

I advise people to have "the courage of their talent." I mean that we all have talent and, if we're cognizant of it, we can use it to provide the courage we need to solicit feedback, ignore unintended slights, and generally improve our condition. We don't have to hide under that rock, we can be vulnerable "in the open."

The courage to connect—to meet the necessity of vulnerability—can come and go. We need to work on the habit or our ability to engage in it can atrophy, especially if our friends, careers, relationships, and circumstances change. Here's what you can do to have the courage to connect at nearly all times and add to your legacy:

- View any question or even objection from a trusted source as a sign of interest and support, not as a degradation. Encourage people you trust to provide you with insights about your behavior and habits.*
- Never act defensively, even if you don't agree with what you're hearing or believe it factually untrue. If the feedback is from a trusted source, simply listen and you can later disregard it. I've told everyone I coach that they should feel free to ignore my advice! That eases the pressure on them.
- Always ask for clarification if you're uncertain about what the advice means. Don't take the risk of ignoring something important or adhering to something unimportant. Clarification is not defensiveness.
- Eschew perfection. Perfectionism kills improvement, because no improvement is ever good enough to create perfection, so people rationalize that it's frustrating to try to improve. Perfectionism is a form of procrastination, which is a greater fear of being critiqued for poor performance than the fear of being critiqued for non-performance!
- Make it three-dimensional whenever possible. Connections are best when you can observe the other person and they observe you. Even modern technology does not allow for full appreciation of body language and eye contact and subtle reactions. (This is especially true when in groups.)

We require vulnerability to learn and to grow. That involves connecting with others we trust, and providing reciprocity in terms of feedback, caring, and support. These are reasonable expectations, and essential to the creation of meaning and our legacy.

---

* One woman I've known for a long time insists that I correct her grammar and pronunciation even in meetings in front of others, that is how much she wants to improve her communications and doesn't have her ego at stake.

CHAPTER 7

The Futility of Ignoring and Avoiding Intimacy

We compete for mates. Why is there such a disproportionate number of beautiful women on the arms of professional male athletes? Why is the divorce rate so high among celebrities? Why does the *Wall Street Journal* have a weekly section on "Mansions"? The competition at the top of society fosters similar behavior down the ladder and is accepted as normal, with "lifestyle" replacing intimacy, the gross revenues of a performance replacing artistic merit, and the manifestation of luxury overwhelming intimacy. (There is also always not just a bigger boat, but a bigger house.)

Of Divorce Rates, Lousy Jobs, and Alienation

If you simply Google divorce rates in the US for first, second, and third marriages, you'll find these rough statistics:

First marriages: 50 percent
Second marriages: 60 percent
Third marriages: 75 percent

Those are not typos. (Some sources question these figures, *but not by* much.) Most people I talk to about this tell me that they'd expect, rationally, that second marriages would be more successful because the parties have learned their lessons, and that third marriages would be the beneficiaries of the education of the first two failed ones.

But this is not the case.

When I talk to clinicians and counselors (and divorce lawyers) about these statistics, they all refer to the same phenomenon.

We keep marrying the exact same people.

And bear in mind that *many* people who should divorce do not. They don't want to bear the immediate pain even though they would avoid longer-term agony. They don't want to suffer the financial consequences. They want to avoid the social stigma. They don't want to disappoint their extended families. (Recall the story of Diana earlier.)

Thus, the actual percentage should probably be higher, not lower, to be realistic.

And why do male professional athletes have a disproportionate number of stunning women as their wives or partners? Because celebrity makes such choices far easier and visible; there's no need to rely on introductions or hang out at bars.

We also endure and tolerate unpleasant and even painful jobs. We suffer under intolerable bosses. Yet when I suggest to people that they divorce their spouse or leave their employer, they tell me it's impossible. And bear in mind that people don't really leave companies, they leave bosses, meaning that the spouse and boss both represent *relationships* that are depressing people or driving them to drink, *yet they fail to do anything to end them.* (I'll quote the humorist George Ade who famously observed, "Don't pity the martyrs, they love the work.")

I realize I'm probably talking to many of you quite intimately right now, and it's intimacy that's at the root of most of this unhappiness.

When we refuse or ignore the need to create meaning we also reject intimacy. "Intimacy" isn't solely or even mainly about sexual relationships, it's about "closeness" and "familiarity." It's about gaining the partners and friends who can provide the honest feedback I discussed in the last chapter.

Case Study: Reporters

I was working with a group of newspaper reporters and editors at the American Press Institute. While discussing communications, a veteran reporter for *The New York Times* said, "Management treats us like lackies. We have old computers, beaten up furniture, low pay, long hours, no respect."

I said, "Why don't you leave?"

He replied, astounded, "What do you mean, 'leave'? I love this work!"

Why do reporters, nurses, teachers, firefighters, and others do outstanding jobs for relatively low pay? Because they're passionate about the work and will put up with a lot of displeasure in order to stay where they are.

Life is too short to be constantly unhappy. Yet many people are. Henry David Thoreau's cynical remark about "most men lead lives of quiet desperation" reflects this frequent condition. We "muddle through," "tolerate," "accept," and "soldier on." We have scores of phrases we use to describe this phenomenon, like the Inuit who have 50 different words to describe "snow." That's how common this dynamic is.

We wind up alienated, with no one really close to us, despite appearances. We don't talk through our problems or truly celebrate our victories. We simply coexist. Think about your own parents, or aunts and uncles, or siblings. Did they, do they, have relationships and friendships which allow for intimate communication and expression?

My contention is that we keep making the same mistakes, traveling the same road rather than try to really improve our route and progress. We hide things from our spouses and partners and refuse to talk back to an unpleasant boss or bully. Our legacy shouldn't be one of "getting by" and "not rocking the boat" and "bearing it." Who would be proud of such a legacy, and who would want to emulate it?

Ask yourself these "forensic" questions about intimacy:

- Am I honest in raising concerns and discomfort with others, or do I subsume my feelings so as not to cause others pain or create awkwardness?
- Do I refuse to share my deepest sentiments and beliefs because I'm afraid of others' reactions?
- Am I enduring long-term pain (or even discomfort) because I'm trying to avoid shorter-term pain which I refuse to bear?
- Do I sometimes feel "alone" with no one to talk to in complete candor? Am I sometimes "alone" even with my family, or my coworkers, or my friends?
- If there were no adverse consequences at all, no one was hurt, would I leave my spouse or partner? Would I leave my current job? Would I change my friends?

Obviously, your answers to these questions also reflect your control or lack of control over your life and work. Moreover, we can't ignore intimacy, we can't run from it. We're often dealing with people who have more power and control than we do because they've embraced intimacy.

I've dealt with hundreds of people far happier after they left their job, their partner, their environments because, for all of the surroundings in which they found themselves, they were still alone.

It takes courage to allow for and engage in intimacy, but intimacy can provide tremendous courage in return.

The Caste System in a New Light

"Caste" has been historically regarded as dividing society into hereditary classes, largely around social privileges. We've seen with social justice movements very recently that caste isn't about "other" cultures, most traditionally associated with the Indian history from Brahmin to "untouchable," but is about our own.[*]

---

[*] Isabel Wilkerson's *Caste: The Origins of Our Discontents* (Penguin Random House 2020) is an excellent investigation of caste, its origins, and its comparisons in India, Nazi Germany, and the US. Neither she nor I believe in the concept of "race."

Castes are formed consciously and unconsciously. If you don't believe that, look at where people generally choose to live—among people like themselves. (That's not solely religious or ethnic, it's also about income and wealth.) Regarding American culture and society, we're finally learning that there is far too much "hereditary" discrimination and not enough equal opportunity.

How ingrained can this become? It's believed the caste system in India was begun in 1500 BC by an influx of Aryan peoples. It was officially banned in 1948, three millennia later, but it still exists unofficially with devastating social harm. Slavery created another caste system in the 1600s in the West, though the practice was common among indigenous peoples in the Caribbean, South America, and Africa, as well. As with India, today we are still dealing with devastating social consequences half a millennium later.

What has this to do with legacy and meaning?

When we allow ourselves to be identified with certain exclusionary social groups, advertently or inadvertently, we are actually reducing intimacy. We are isolating ourselves among people who have similar backgrounds, similar accomplishments, similar beliefs. One of the most vivid examples of caste is background or origin, in that there are clubs and experiences that many people are denied because of those factors. Although we look like the people who belong, we're denied entry, not always because of monetary differences, but because of who our grandparents were. I've met many people with brilliant façades who are actually impoverished. But their names, inherited, carry weight with others like them.

The "new light" I'm referring to in terms of caste* is that of finding meaning through broad experiences and a wide variety of friends and relationships. Perhaps counterintuitively, "intimacy" is not merely about becoming close and being vulnerable to those with whom you are most comfortable. It is about being so with those who are not so similar.

My travels to over 60 countries have demonstrated to me that all of us in the human community are far more similar than dissimilar. We generally

---

* I know this is an emotionally laden word, which is why I'm using it to discuss legacy.

share the same sense of humor, enjoy the same art forms, need love, and accept personal responsibility. We all have our saints and we all have our criminals and sins.

However, it's the much smaller aspect of dissimilarity that's important to experience. If we're merely intimate with those who are similar to us, we learn very little. If we solely "open up" to those who share our experiences and emotions we receive commiseration but not growth.

Thus, it's vital to our creation of meaning that we "expose" ourselves to diverse others and welcome them into our embrace. That allows us to broaden meaning and to create a larger, more meaningful legacy.

Case Study: Merck

When "diversity" and "inclusiveness" were first introduced with urgency into American business decades ago, all kinds of training and studies were performed. Managers received "diversity training" and were sent on their way, "cured" of any biases. However, many (or, perhaps, most) biases are hidden and subconscious.

In the late 1990s the pharmaceutical giant Merck asked me to conduct a baseline diversity study. I had worked with them for many years and they trusted me, and I knew the organization quite well. At the time it was in the midst of being cited as "America's Most Admired Company" by the annual *Fortune Magazine* poll of executives.

Merck was stunned when I found that Asian employees were told they could never go into management, only research, because they "couldn't confront" people. Immigrants were told they couldn't advance because of their accents (they were fluent and perfectly understandable). Racial jokes and epithets were common amidst small groups.

When senior management had trouble accepting my report, I brought them to the huge cafeteria and asked them what they saw.

It took several minutes before they realized that people seemed to be self-segregating into different parts of the huge room.

After that, Merck stopped "training" people in diversity and started changing behavior through coaching, role models, and the occasional termination of the unalterably biased.

I've explained all this to arrive at this point for you, personally: What are you doing to avoid promulgating a caste mentality in your own life, in your own meaning, in your own legacy? The entire concept of "legacy" admissions to elite schools is appalling to me. Why should someone receive preferential treatment just because a parent attended the school? Why shouldn't they have to qualify like everyone else? (And I'm not even attempting to discuss the arrogance of bribing and lying to get your kids into schools, which entertainment celebrities and business executives attempted quite recently and are being jailed for as I write this.)

No one deserves anything purely because of parentage, nor should someone be denied anything purely because of parentage. Similarly, we shouldn't limit our creation of meaning by acting within an ephemeral kind of "community" of nearly identical people. But that is too often the natural default condition.

Therefore, we need to open up our community, including our vulnerability and search for intimacy, to a wider range of people and experiences. That requires a conscious effort, a deliberate effort, and a continuing effort. Otherwise, we can find ourselves in that same cafeteria, enjoying common food but solely with people like ourselves.

How bad can that get? Consider the McMansion Syndrome.

The McMansion Syndrome

I love reading the *Wall Street Journal* but I've always been puzzled by their extra section one day a week labeled "Mansions." Therein we find some shocking examples of over-indulgence. Don't misunderstand, I'm a capitalist and believe in the rewards of hard work. However, I also believe that the disparity of executive pay in relation to average worker pay in most organizations is ridiculous.

If you found a company (Fred Smith, Bill Gates, Joan and George Johnson, Steve Jobs, Richard Branson*) you deserve whatever money that endeavor provides you. In many cases, that will be zero, because most start-ups fail. There should be commensurate reward for substantial risk.

However, if you are appointed to be CEO of a publicly held company, whether from the inside or the outside, there should be a limit on pay. Really, does a $150 million a year package produce a better result than an executive making a tenth of that? How much money do you need? And it's not always about salary. Jeff Immelt, who drove GE into the ground as CEO, was only paid about $4 million a year, but received a retirement package of over $200 million. His successor, Larry Culp, receives only half Immelt's salary (about $2 million) but has bonus potential of $4 million and another $15 million in "equity compensation."

Thomas Alva Edison founded GE, and he deserved whatever he made because he invented what the company sold.

Thus, back to my McMansions.

Capitalism creates wealth very efficiently, but it is lousy at distributing wealth efficiently. That is, there are societal needs and individual needs which any civilized people must attend to, from paving the roads to health care, from preventing crime to providing education. Dostoevsky said, "If you want to judge the values of a society, try entering its prisons."

Capitalism is about a country's trade and business being in private hands. Socialism is about ownership controlled by the state, which is why these two positions are so polarized. Historically, socialism has not succeeded, largely because it has always resulted in oligarchy, where a few privileged people rule everyone else. But any system can suffer when it leads to extremes.

And we have an extreme in wealth and poverty in America.

---

* FedEx, Microsoft, Johnson Products, Apple, Virgin Atlantic.

Not everyone reads the *Wall Street Journal* but that "Mansions" section is disturbing to me. It highlights that extreme which undermines capitalist society. How many houses does one need? At this writing, singer Taylor Swift has eight homes valued at over $81 million. How big a yacht do you need? The late Paul Allen, cofounder of Microsoft, paid $325 million for his yacht. Swift and Tylor are not traditional corporate executives, of course, but they do represent the conspicuous consumption that infects our society.

The mansions that the *Journal* cites each week routinely have 10,000 or more square feet, a movie-viewing room, ten or more bedrooms with private baths, 50,000 gallon and larger pools, eight-car garages—even a helipad. And these are homes often owned by present and former corporate executives, not solely entertainers and entrepreneurs. It's one thing to win the lottery and use your winnings as you like. But it's another to work for a company that is owned by investors and make far more than they ever will.

In all fairness, many of these people are philanthropic and support public initiatives. However, the question remains: Does a $100 million CEO run a company better than, say, a $20 million CEO? There is no evidence to support this. And should a CEO make up to 1,000 times the income of the average worker? I see no reason why this should ever be the case.

What do the McMansions and excessive compensation have to do with legacy?

We should be thinking about wealth and accomplishment and lifestyle in different ways than we see in the McMansions section, or among "celebrities," or even among business tycoons. I would remind you that Warren Buffet, the smartest investment guy of all time and worth billions, drives a 2014 Cadillac. And while the car's cost of $45,000 isn't chicken liver, it's only a tenth of the price of a Rolls Royce.

We have come to equate success with requiring certain manifestations, whether clothing or jewelry, vacation homes or private schools. Yet none of that is legacy, and it has precious little meaning. That's simply what money can buy. But our calling, our passion, can't be the pursuit of money, although it may well be a by-product.

We should be pursuing happiness. We should be pursuing contribution. We should be pursuing accountability.

The question is about what metrics we decide to use. Do we crave to be seen in the house with ten bedrooms and on the deck of a seven-figure yacht, or do we pursue support of others, philanthropy, contribution to the environment, and raising our kids well? What money can provide us is the discretionary time to spend on these endeavors, and that is real wealth. Money is simply fuel. And you don't even need the fuel to take time to help your kids with their homework, or celebrate an anniversary, or volunteer at a food kitchen, or rescue animals from shelters.

If there is a McMansion in your life, let it be in your soul.

Luxury Tends to Mask Intimacy

Something is a luxury until we use it once and it contributes to our well-being in some way. That could be physically, emotionally, spiritually, or mentally. No one was demanding a remote garage door opener or remote TV control. Why would we need proximity indicators and cameras mounted around cars? I mentioned earlier Henry Ford's observation that his potential customers would have requested faster horses.

That woman I mentioned who sold me an early car phone presented me with such an option. Not long after, once the phone was a "necessity" and not a novelty (that took about four hours) I was finishing a call to London from the car and complained to my wife about too much static on the call.

"Alan!" she admonished, "you're calling *London from your car!* Stop complaining!"

We tend to make this trip from the new and exciting to the routine and required very rapidly. We are all "early adapters" when something can immediately improve our well-being and it doesn't hurt! Thus, buying a large-screen TV or an electric toothbrush is easy, but using new gym equipment or utilizing more modern dentistry is not. Telling me that shovel is more ergonomic doesn't motivate me to start digging.

We acclimate ourselves to luxury quickly, but this can get in the way of intimacy. The luxury and modernization and greater comfort all help us avoid, not achieve, intimacy and connection.

The reasons for this are as obvious as a ham sandwich:

- We don't need to be present to deal with people, even loved ones. We can use the omnipresent smart phone, FaceTime, text, email, Instagram, and whatever else comes along by the time you read this. While I'm the first to admit these can increase intimacy when one is a soldier assigned overseas or on a prolonged business trip, these devices are employed locally in place of direct contact. I've seen (as have you) people text and call from one part of a house to another, or from adjoining cubicles in an office.

- We have made the devices the center of our attention rather than what they can do to help us. How many times have you seen a family sit down in a restaurant for breakfast or dinner and watched all four people submerge into an iPhone or iPad? The waitstaff usually has to interrupt them. I watched a video of four people in a gondola in Venice all staring at their phones instead of the history just yards away.

- We allow and endorse "dropping out" of conversation and interactions—and intimacy. Parents allow a child to submerge into a device while with them in order to avoid painful questions, disruptive behavior, and/or whining. It becomes a modern "pacifier" right up through teenage years.

- We become engulfed by the noise of the internet and the gallimaufry of opinions, facts, biases, and rants that are equally blasted in the public square. We feel we're "connecting" with others through "likes, reactions, followers, shares," and so on, but we're merely fish in the school mindlessly swimming though the ocean without direction or cause.

- We use material possessions as a metric of success and they frequently isolate us. We are frequently in vacation properties, personal homes, recreational locations, school, and entertainment venues where we are actually isolated. We see people only like ourselves and we behave like lemmings. Moreover, we mistakenly think we're in contact with each other in these conditions, but we're really not. We're simply engaged in shared, narrow experiences.

These are the some of the reasons why we mistake luxury for success and achievement *and meaning*. There is always a bigger boat (TIAABB). You'll never have the largest, and that shouldn't be the point or the pursuit.

This is also why "remote learning" is so desperately inadequate, though it is being hyped as a modern approach to learning. On a business or self-development basis, there is little or no peer learning involved, especially if one is taking courses based solely on completing modules independently. The drop-out rate is high, the learning is not solidified by an instructor or facilitator, and the ensuing skills aren't fully understood or applied.

Would you like a surgeon to operate on you who went through online learning to gain a degree? Or a lawyer to represent you in court? Or an architect to design your home? Or a consultant to give you business advice?

As I write this we are in huge debates about online learning in schools during periods of disease and illness. My experience is that this is as unfulfilling and ineffective as any other kind of online learning. This is because:

- Virtually no teachers are prepared to do it well.
- It requires the attention of a parent to supplement it, and most parents are too busy working to provide the time (which is far more than merely reviewing homework assignments).
- Distractions are far too frequent and alluring.
- It's difficult to provide individualized attention to those who can move more swiftly and those who require more time.
- *Socialization is completely absent. Schools provide social experience and correction as much as academic instruction. Online learning is actually "desocializing."*

For all of these reasons and in all these conditions luxury interferes with intimacy, which decreases meaning, which undermines legacy. If we want to create legacy, and not just "borrow" it from someone else using their metrics, then we can't ignore intimacy.

We have to overcome these barriers to it by communicating in real time, in the presence of others. We can't allow our families to "opt-out" into technology or to substitute virtual for real.

We need to be in contact and connected every day.

CHAPTER 8

Extremism Is Mindless Competition's Illegitimate Spawn

If we weren't so competitive we wouldn't cheat so much, and we wouldn't find so many ingenious ways to cheat. The Nazis tried to rig the 1936 Olympics, Rosie Ruiz took the subway to try to win the New York Marathon, and drug testing is now a standard accompaniment of all major sports. We cheat because "winning" has become mindlessly addictive, even in cutting a line to board a plane or sneaking into the members-only airline club. A Harvard rowing coach who was asked about his team's finish in last place in the Olympics commented, "Since when is there anything to be ashamed about by being eighth best in the world?"

From Armstrong to McGwire and Back

Neil Armstrong walked on the moon in 1969, fulfilling John F. Kennedy's promise that we would do that "within the decade." Although President Kennedy was assassinated not long after his prediction, the full weight and momentum of that intent carried through.

Armstrong happened to be the right person in the right sequence with the right background to be the first of several who would follow. He was continually humble about the accomplishment and led as normal a life as he could. He hadn't bribed anyone to gain the honor, he hadn't cheated on any tests, and he didn't personally exploit the result.

Mark McGwire hit 70 home runs in 1998, in a consistent improvement over Babe Ruth's legendary 60 (in 1927), a record that had stood, impregnable, for 34 years. Subsequently, McGwire's record was broken by Sammy Sosa at 73.

However, in retirement, McGwire admitted to what many had long suspected: prolonged steroid use, a banned, performance-improving substance, over the course of his career. Twenty years later, he still has not been inducted into the Major League Baseball Hall of Fame®.

We witness many subjective awards, evaluations, and wins and losses in life: entertainment awards, figure skating judging, gymnastics judging, dance contests, singing competitions, even the Pulitzer and Nobel Prizes, which are often more political than justifiable. It's interesting that some truly objective awards, such as valedictorian, based on grades, have been abandoned to preserve those non-deserving of it their "self-worth." (In fact, it does the opposite. No one proudly shows a "participation award" to others, not if you don't want to be laughed out of the room.) Remember all those colleges that went to "pass/fail," the progressive Ivy League schools most notably? They didn't want to discriminate among those who studied hard and excelled and those who simply muddled through.

I believe it was the legendary Kentucky basketball coach Adolph Rupp who said, "If the outcome doesn't matter, why does anyone bother to keep score?" My son told me once, while playing such a "no score" game in grammar school, "We all knew who was winning and by how much."

There are some dynamics, apparently, that are unassailable in our ability to see where we stand, how successful or unsuccessful we've been. The stock market comes to mind. We can see our investments appreciate or deteriorate. We can measure that in the morning stock results. It's an "Armstrong" moment: We are walking on the moon or failing to reach it.

But, wait: Here comes Bernie Madoff, promising unheard-of returns in an economy that doesn't justify them. And people begin throwing money. At parties in Palm Beach even the conservative, "old-line" monied people would beg Bernie to take their money.

And he did.

I think every person who lost money in Madoff's Ponzi scheme through the errors of their investment advisors should be reimbursed for that foolishness. But every person who *independently* chose to give Madoff money should not be. Everyone should have known better, most people suspected he was crooked, *but they figured they could make money anyway because he wasn't getting caught and they didn't need to know any more than that.*

Extremism arises when we feel we're at a disadvantage and can't legitimately compete. This happens with governments, companies (Volkswagen and emissions), teams (the New England Patriots, six-time Super Bowl winners, have been penalized for unfair practices), and individuals (see Rosie Ruiz in the next section). Entire prep schools have distorted grades upwards to ensure their graduates get into the best colleges, thus protecting their desirability and high tuitions.

Infamously, presidential candidate Barry Goldwater said that "extremism in defense of liberty is no vice," and promptly lost the election in a landslide to Lyndon B. Johnson. Extremism is always a vice, and is mindless competition's illegitimate spawn.

By "illegitimate" I mean that the competition is based on winning no matter what the cost, repute, or risk. The meaning we seek to create must originate in a greater universe than simply "winning" no matter what. But "winning" has become such a strong motivator, such an important part of one's persona, that the ends justify almost any means.

"Winning" also often means "beating the system," evading taxes, securing preferential treatment with a bribe, and walking into a club of which you're not a member. Watching people sneak into airline clubs in airports is an exercise in watching the cheaters who would rather take advantage of everyone else than pay for what they're taking.

I always turn them in.

Maybe Rosie Ruiz Was Right

Rosie Ruiz was the declared winner of the 84th Boston Marathon, among women entrants, in 1980. Eight days later her title was stripped when it was determined she had entered the race about a half-hour before the finish! No one seemed to notice at the time that she hadn't perspired, her muscles weren't toned like a marathoner's, and she couldn't remember parts of the course.

What people don't generally know was that she had previously run the New York Marathon and finished 11th among women, quite respectable. After the Boston disqualification, New York officials found that she had not run that entire race either, and retroactively disqualified her. It turns out she took the subway to a point near the finish line and identified herself as an injured runner.

Ms. Ruiz was born in Havana and emigrated to the US. After the Boston race, she wound up in Florida, and was arrested twice, once for embezzlement and once for dealing in cocaine. Both sentences were light with little jail time. She died in 2019 at age 66 of cancer.

Rosie Ruiz is an historical figure not unlike the cheating scandal on the old "64,000 Question" TV show where the contest was rigged ahead of time to determine who won. One of those contestants was Dr. Joyce Brothers, who went on to fame as one of the most notable celebrity psychologists. (Her specialty was the category of boxing.) There were the eight members of the Chicago "Black Sox" (White Sox) who conspired to lose the 1919 World Series.

In more modern times, we see TV ratings distorted, illegal performance drugs in sports, and outright cheating in stealing tests in schools and hacking into the system to change grades.

What strikes me, however, is that a lot of the cheaters and criminals get their day in the sun, the 15 minutes that Andy Warhol foresaw for everyone. Rosie Ruiz was interviewed and gained some evanescent fame. She might have created some worthwhile life out of her experience and insights but she didn't. The circus around the original O.J. Simpson trial created huge media investment, book deals, and mini-series for many years, and made household names out of non-entities in many cases.

Of course, what it didn't produce was justice.

We distort meaning by too often chasing the wrong things. We don't seek originality, but rather we become derivative. Two authors I know, Jack Canfield and Mark Victor Hansen, compiled *Chicken Soup for the Soul* in

1993, and have since created a merchandising monster around it. They were very clever marketers.

However, soon after the book became a hit, every man and his dog (as the Australians are fond of saying) began trying to create similar works—compilations of clever sayings and adages to help people through the day. I was besieged with people asking me for my favorite stories and experiences for such prospective works as *Nourishment for Your Pet* (I kid you not). All of these were stark attempts to cash in on Canfield's and Hansen's good idea, and all failed. (If you contributed to them, you had to sign a legal document giving up all rights to your own stories!)

Meaning isn't derivative, which is why I scorn "searching for meaning" as if it's a buried treasure or resides in some fossilized guru high in the Himalayas conversing with the Yeti.

I've never cared about feedback forms and ratings when I speak or write or consult or coach. (And, therefore, I've never been moved to "rig" them, as I've seen many people do in order to boast of "high ratings.") My "meaning" is that I've prepared well, shown up on time, done my very best, and gone home happy. I'm not vulnerable to some human resources person gathering ridiculous feedback sheets that ask about the food, the lighting, and the speaker.

Case Study: The Car Dealership

There is a huge car dealership near me owned by a single family for generations. When you buy the car the sales person will ask you (and when serviced, the service manager will ask you) to give them all "10s" on the ensuing survey "or we won't get a full bonus." That's called "managing the survey," and the dealership does that to get the highest ratings which will give it preferential treatment from the manufacturer.

The dealership service is quite good, and the cars are fine. But they can't let it rest there, the owners have to cheat to come out on top.

I'm responsible to myself. And so I ask you:

- Do you have your own metrics for success? Do you know when you've performed well, not reliant on the arbitrary feedback of others?
- Are you capable of judging your performance beyond external input? I've done excellent jobs in front of people who couldn't be moved with a thousand-pound bomb because they were unhappy with their own management, and I've been praised to the skies by people who had been subject to two prior days of boring presentations and I was fresh air. You have to parse out your own performance.
- Are you in the kind of competitions I've discussed throughout the book that really are unsubstantial and irrelevant and ought to be abandoned? Maybe you don't belong in a marathon but rather in a program coaching aspiring writers.[*]
- Are you overly swayed by the limelight others derive in their fields and advertently or inadvertently try to emulate them?

Rosie Ruiz was right in trying to "be someone," especially as an immigrant who may have experienced prejudice in her life. But she chose *not* to be someone as Rosie Ruiz, but to be someone else.

That's the antithesis to the creation of personal meaning.

The Boys in the Boat

The Boys in the Boat (Daniel James Brown, Penguin Random House, 2014) is a book about nine men who won a rowing contest at the 1936 Berlin Olympics, against all odds, and against the Nazis' every effort to "rig" the race, no less than Rosie Ruiz's attempts at a stolen victory. They were the University of Washington's crew team, and these were not Ivy League rich

---

[*] I've known a lot of people who trained like crazy, with great discipline, and succeeded in an athletic competition; however, that success didn't help their personal or professional lives one whit.

kids, but rather hard-working men who needed part-time jobs and scholarships to get through school.

If you're not familiar with crew, it's a grueling sport, with practices often held in icy waters and strong winds in the very early morning, with bleeding hands and sore backs, with complete exhaustion as the inevitable result in every contest.

There are a lot of these stories. The movie *Rudy* depicted a struggling, under-talented athlete who managed to play for Notre Dame through sheer perseverance and determination. A more recent book, *Faster* (Neal Bascomb, Houghton Mifflin Harcourt, 2020), tells a story of a Jewish driver winning a Grand Prix race otherwise dominated by Germans of the Nazi Party in the late 1930s.

Such historical "drama" is important because we learn that the "underdog" can win against huge odds, and that talent and determination can win out. That's not always the case, of course. In fact, it's rarely the case. Jesse Owens won the sprints in those 1936 Olympics because he was the fastest, greatest runner of his time, and you can't "fix" a sprint. But otherwise, we're back with Voltaire and "heaviest, best shooting battalions."

But we're also back to that Harvard coach who said there's nothing wrong with being the eighth-best rowing team in the world. And even that is questionable, since we've discussed the fallacy of hundredths of an inch and thousandths of a second. There really is no "best" at any particular point in time in a universal, totally objective sense. There is simple a concatenation of events that allow certain performers to arrive in certain places at certain times, where they are successful against other performers who arrived in certain places at certain times. The performers are "best" in that particular moment, but not universally or fundamentally.

There is no way to tell who's "best" on a global scale for any particular competition, only ways to determine who survived prior competitions to arrive at a final reckoning against others. Sports championships are often settled by the best three of five or four of seven. Before they introduced the Van Allen tennis tie-braker, sets could go on for days until decided. Was one player "better" than the other, or simply more of a survivor than athlete?

Think of the marriage statistics I presented earlier. Is the perfect mate for you, among six billion inhabitants of the planet, really someone you went to school with, or met on a vacation, or was introduced to by a friend? Or was this person a wonderful match for you at that moment without an exhaustive search for someone even better that might have taken years?! I'm not denigrating young love, I'm simply pointing out that we live our lives with the mistaken belief we're seeing the best and the perfect, when we're really experiencing the good and the acceptable.

We tend to engage in extremism to guide us in the pursuit of certain ideals, yet not others. We believe that some disciplines require endless practice (basketball, surgery, the piano) while others rely on visceral reactions to guide us (romance, hobbies, professions). Both are a kind of extremism, however, in that believing that we've found something perfect in a relationship or "calling" is no different from believing we have to practice endlessly to master a trade or any endeavor.

Malcom Gladwell, an author I admire, researches his books meticulously in my view (though some critics claim he "cherry picks" his research to support his conclusions). He has claimed that it takes 10,000 hours of practice (perhaps metaphorically) for great talent to emerge, whether an athlete or an entertainer or a professional. However, I don't believe that Michael Jordan, or Frank Sinatra, or Louis Armstrong, or Meryl Streep, or Bill Gates needed all those hours. Gladwell is trying to make a case for extremism in gaining perfection.

But my point is that life is about success, not perfection.

While there are examples of people who perform "at the top of their game" for most of their careers, that's not the point of meaning, as great as their legacies might be. It's fascinating and incredible to continue to listen to Sinatra sing The Great American Songbook today, better than anyone ever has and probably ever will. It's impressive to consider how Michael Jordan and Tiger Woods changed their respective games, and how many young people they inspired.

But meaning is not about universal acclaim or endless practice. It is organic, not a destination. That is, it's part of our living present, part of that book we're writing every day, not a goal to reach or obstacle to surmount, or competition to win through talent and determination.

Case Study: Philippe Petit

Philippe Petit was a high-wire performer who walked the wire between the New York City World Trade Center towers in 1974 (and the spires of Notre Dame in 1971). A documentary was made of his achievement, which I aired as chairman of the Newport International Film Festival in 2008. Mr. Petit, then in his 50s, was invited and was kind enough to join us and answer questions for the audience.

During the cocktail reception that night, I realized he was not present. I found him out on the docks, staring into the dark night and placid waters. And I realized in talking to him that there was nothing else for him. His big moment had passed, he was too old to do more, and he had no further meaning in his life.

He was far lonelier standing on that dock than walking in the sky over lower Manhattan, 1,300 feet above ground.

Hence, meaning is not a one-time achievement, or even a succession of victories. It is a state of mind that embraces you and which you embrace. It represents your legacy.

The Desert Isle for the Exiled

The legendary and somewhat curmudgeonly news anchor, David Brinkley, once remarked that the dictators Idi Amin and Muammar Gaddafi should both be arrested and exiled to a remote island in the Pacific. He recommended that just the two of them live there, share their meals, and after dinner each night they could play gin rummy—and both cheat.

I fell on the floor at the stark, dark humor in that.

We need to "exile" the extremes of mindless competition to a remote and distant part of our world. Otherwise, meaning becomes all tangled up with achievement, and achievement is transmogrified into "winning." And winning does mean that you come out on top, *and that the other person also has to lose because the others are "inferior."*

Hence, polarization and moral narcissism prevail.

Neil Armstrong wasn't competing to be the first on the moon nor even the first out of the module. He simply followed his passion and did the best he possibly could. His meaning probably wasn't *Star Trek*'s "go where no man has gone before," but it was to "push the envelope" and explore whatever was possible in his field.

Rosie Ruiz wasn't trying to create meaning, she was trying to steal it by being someone she wasn't. And like most people in that category, she was easily found out. Bernie Madoff took longer to be exposed but that, too, was inevitable. Every Ponzi scheme is inevitably exposed, except for the blissfully naïve. Mark McGwire and countless other athletes who have cheated and were seeking fame, not meaning.

When Ted Williams, the Hall-of-Fame Red Sox outfielder, was batting just over .400 for the season, his manager, Joe Cronin, another Hall-of-Famer, offered to pull him from the lineup for the final game of the season, since if he went hitless he would dip under .400. Williams wouldn't hear of it, went six-for-eight in a doubleheader, and wound up the season at .401. That was 80 years ago, and no one has done it since.

The boys in the boat were simply engaged in their passion, competitive rowing, and were trying to do the best they could. They didn't complain about the poorer equipment compared to Ivy League standards, or the harsh practice conditions of the Pacific Northwest, or of the assignment to a much tougher lane by the Nazi officials in the Olympic finals. And they didn't lord it over the Germans when they had won. They simply did their best, found their meaning, relished in that meaning, and created their legacy.

What does this mean for us?

As you write you book of life each day, consider these tenets about meaning and worth:

- You don't have to be the best, you simply have to consistently do the best you're capable of doing.
- Losing isn't a sin or a crime. If you learn from setbacks and defeats, you're moving forward, nonetheless.
- You *can* cheat your way to the front or the top, but you'll be caught eventually and that's not meaning but a dearth of meaning.
- You can't create meaning "trying not to lose," you create it by trying your best to succeed. That's the Ted Williams lesson.
- It is sufficient that you "win" when appropriate and possible, but not mandatory that the other person "lose." Gracious winners embrace their competitors, they don't "showboat."
- Meaning is a journey, not an ending. Legacy is continual, not final.

But as you'll soon see, you don't always have to stay in the lead.

CHAPTER 9

So What If Someone's Gaining on You?

We become paranoid about "being caught from behind," and adhere to mindless admonitions about discipline and focus lest we're surprised by someone highly unlikely passing us by. In law firms it's "up or out," in universities "publish or perish," on New Hampshire license plates, "live free or die." Isn't there some comfortable middle ground here? Legacy is daily, you don't have to worry about someone beating you to the finish line or even beating you to the punch.

The Early Worm Gets Eaten

We become inured with sayings and wisdom and parables to the point that they become mindless guides of our lives. What was supposed to have profound meaning now loses meaning. And for every suggested action there is an equal and opposite suggested action.

Some examples:

- Opposites attract. Birds of a feather flock together.
- All good things come to those who wait. A stitch in time saves nine.
- Clothes make the person. You cannot judge a book by its cover.
- Familiarity breeds contempt. Home is where the heart is.

- Laugh and the world laughs with you; weep and you weep alone. Misery loves company.
- Early to bed, early to rise, makes a man healthy, wealthy, and wise. Eat drink and be merry for tomorrow we may die.
- Absence makes the heart grow fonder. Out of sight, out of mind.
- The early bird gets the worm. Haste makes waste.

I'm writing this part of the book in a beach house on Nantucket Island. The studio where I write looks out over an expanse of lawn to the ocean. Early in the mornings the robins visit the lawn to feast on an abundance of worms. The early birds get the worms, *but the early worms get eaten.*

We are too consumed by "words of wisdom" which actually seem intended to justify about any action and validate all behaviors. "Take your time," but "life is short." I love the Army's informal doctrine: "Hurry up and wait!"

Dizzy Dean, the one-time outstanding and eccentric baseball pitcher, is famed for having said, "Don't look back, someone may be gaining on you." But who cares? We're admonished by motivational speakers to look out the windshield not the rearview mirror, and watch the boat's bow not its wake. (Motivational speakers are themselves an oxymoron, since motivation is intrinsic and one person cannot motivate another. However, anyone can spew platitudes!)

Meaning isn't about winning; it's about understanding who you are and what you can contribute daily—your legacy. It's not even about competing with yourself, let alone others. Counterintuitively, I think it's important to look in all directions: back in appreciation and perspective, forward in anticipation and eagerness, but primarily around you, today, in awareness. We are so consumed with preparing for tomorrow and regretting things we've done in the past (or re-celebrating old "victories") that we aren't connected to the world around us in the present. To me, this connectivity is true "spirituality," divorced from the religious context, and I'll come back to it at the end of this chapter.

We lead our lives as if running a race—against our prior performance, against others, against time in general. We all see people oblivious to the world around them, immersed in the screen of a mobile device, unaware of their surroundings and colleagues. So what if someone is gaining on you? Do you need to be "teacher of the year" or "employee of the month" or win some meaningless award granted by people who merely hand out awards?

There are numerous "Who's Who" organizations, one of which began as listings of people of true wealth and prominence, but which were mainly informal agreed-upon lists of "movers and shakers." But in accordance with the engine of crass commercialism, "Who's Who" books began "selling" inclusion. You all know this, admit it. You'd be "chosen" by the editors for Who's Who in:

- Northeastern Business
- Powerful Women
- Successes Under Forty

You get the idea. The "catch" was that you needed to buy the resultant book for $350 or so, and you were encouraged to buy extra copies for your friends and family. There was even a Who's Who of Pets, which was especially popular, since people will spend anything on their pets.*

These are all rip-offs, an attempt to take your money for an artificial endorsement that "no one is gaining on you." Whenever I see a "Who's Who" mention on a résumé I immediately dismiss the candidate as someone who is shallow and unsophisticated and thinks they can take the "Rosie Ruiz shortcut" to the finish line.

The early bird may be fed first, but the early worm is food first. It's not always the best to follow the adages, apothems, and platitudes. Meaning doesn't require that you be first, or that you stay in the lead, or that you prevent anyone from gaining on you.

Meaning is about who you are, not where you are.

---

* I almost managed to get my dog, Trotsky, into the human "Who's Who" until they demanded a check or credit card in his name. And he was going to buy ten books!

Rushing through the Open Gate

I've had the pleasure of living with seven dogs over the past 30 years or so. I admire their spirit and their *joie de vivre*. There are dog-specific traits, such as a great sense of smell and outstanding hearing. There are breed-specific traits, such as a Beagle's extraordinary sense of smell, the retrieving abilities of a Labrador, and the delight in working of a German Shepherd.

Then there are dog-specific traits. My first white German Shepherd,* Koufax, would not retrieve a thing, and would simply stare at anything thrown wondering how you intended to recapture it. My second white German Shepherd, Bentley, will retrieve anything thrown and has his own stash of sticks behind the tree line in the backyard just in case you fail to bring something with you. He will drop one on a guest's ankles and stare expectantly. If you don't react, he will repeat the gesture, harder, on the assumption you have a learning disability.

One thing that is dog-specific in my experience is that almost all normal dogs will run out through an open gate. They do not perform a risk analysis, they do not go partway through and wait for what might occur, they do not hesitate—they run through the gate no less than Circe lured hapless sailors into her clutches. Running to daylight, as the great football coach Vince Lombardi once called it, is the crack cocaine for dogs.

That is not a human-specific trait by any means. We see new territory (isn't the grass always greener over there—see the final chapter of this book) and hesitate. We assign more risk than reward to the excursion. And an excursion it is, because if we sally forth it will be at a controlled speed with care and consideration, with baggage and bearers, with a cautious mien.

And we want to know how the gate got open, because it's an even bet that it's a trap.

Creating meaning *demands* that we run through the gate if it's open, and tear it down if it's closed. We hear a great deal about "thinking outside

---

* These are not albinos, but simply white dogs and, if they were a separate breed, would be about the 16th most popular in the country.

of the box," *but we can't think outside of the box if we don't get out of the box.* There is no teleportation of our thinking.

That "open gate" is a metaphor for escaping our stultified mentality, our daily grind, our ongoing, meaningless competitions. We all become "corralled" or "barricaded" in our thinking and lives. The most passionately diversity-minded still tend to live with, work with, and commune with people like themselves. We accept values and beliefs from those around us through normative pressure.

To create meaning, we can't tread water or run in place. *A treadmill gives you a workout but not a journey.* Too many of our lives, as fast-paced as we perceive them, are on treadmills. We scoff at the hamster at our own expense. The hamster expects no forward movement, is not trying to create meaning, but merely to while away the time and work off its last meal.

What represents our open gates, or how do we open the gates?

- We have to travel and meet new people in other lands and other conditions. We can't experience the world through the History Channel or National Geographic. I've been to 63 countries, and I speak from experience. Both my xenophobia and my arrogance disappeared when I realized Galileo was right, not Ptolemy.

- We have to deliberately keep adding to or replacing our circle of friends. Lifelong friends may be valuable, but we grow at different speeds in differing ways, and they are actually "anchors" at times. We need "transient" friends who come and go as we grow. Some may hang around, some may not. The star football quarterback, Michael Vick, had to serve jail time for organizing dog fighting in his multi-million-dollar home, because he had never moved on from his early friends.

- We have to expose ourselves to new and often painful points of view. F. Scott Fitzgerald observed that intellect is the ability to hold two conflicting thoughts in one's mind at the same time. This is the antithesis of the polarized, morally narcissistic society in which we currently reside.

- We need to challenge our own beliefs, no matter how long or deeply held. They may have been helpful at one point, but as we grow so do our needs and values.

The creation of meaning is the accumulation of our deliberate actions to change, experience, grow, and evolve. We do that best by running through the metaphorically open gate, or by tearing it down.

When we had yards with no gate, or gates that were never open, our dogs dug under them or some jumped over them.

Managing Your Time

Live free or die, publish or perish, "up or out": These are great pressures on our time. DO SOMETHING! DON'T JUST STAND THERE!

Why? Why not just stand there for a while?

Sometimes you have to slow down to speed up. I coach people in sales meetings to take their time building a trusting relationship. The more time you invest in doing so, the faster the proposal phase will go later because the buyer will feel comfortable disclosing information due to that trust established earlier.

We've all been in situations where we didn't take the time to read the instructions carefully, and wound up with a few parts left over after we thought the assembly was completed.

If we live our lives in fear that someone is "gaining on us," or that we're falling farther behind someone in front of us, our time is not our own. It belongs to the people and dynamics around us. People work 80-hour weeks to become a partner in a firm because they're trying to obtain and sustain the top position. I'm sure you've known quite a few "workaholics" in your life. I've found that even after they've made partner or gained whatever position they've sacrificed for, they don't let up.

Their mania is an ingrained habit, and the hours never diminish.

Case Study: The Workaholic CEO

I was working with the CEO of a half-billion-dollar firm who was working about 70 hours a week and often on Saturdays. He was a chemist who became an executive, a scientist who turned strategist. Just as he worked manically in the lab, he worked manically in the corner office.

He told me his wife was extremely unhappy, and I suggested we realistically reduce his week to 60 hours, meaning 7 am to 7 pm daily, with no Saturdays. He would be home by about 7:45 pm. He arose at 5:30 in the morning in any case. I realized that a 25 percent reduction in hours was the most we could reasonably obtain at the moment.

He was skeptical, but I explained that *time is a priority, not a resource*. That means that he could *reallocate* time from low priorities and low-return issues to those of much greater import and impact. He agreed to try.

Within a month we had reached our goal, abandoning some tasks altogether and delegating others of low importance. He told me, "My wife thinks you're a miracle worker, we have dinner every night together and I'm home all weekend."

Time is a priority, not a resource. We all have 24 hours in a day. We all know of our non-negotiable requirements: sleep, medical care, family, entertainment, and so forth. Yet some of us begin to whittle away at those when we feel we need to accomplish more. We don't have dinner with the family, we don't exercise, we cancel medical checkups, we eschew vacations. And we sleep less.

But if you appreciate that time is a *priority* which can be assigned and reallocated, you have a completely different dynamic. One major example would be meetings. Most meetings are useless, they are exchanges of information which could be done electronically, or gatherings where one has to be "seen," or excuses for people to exercise their egos with meaningless speeches and irrelevant comments.

Does that sound harsh? Well, consider your own experiences. We waste a huge part of our lives in meetings, including virtual meetings. Just because you can do it doesn't mean you should. And senior people are as guilty as anyone else. (Imagine if sales people in the streets, or assembly line workers, or teachers, were in hours of meetings daily. Productivity and performance would go down the drain.)

Take a look at your time, and ignore who may be gaining on you. What are your real priorities, what is the important *meaning* in your life? That's where your time should go. And if you find you don't have "enough" time, then *take if from somewhere else* and don't try to "create" it by sleeping less or sacrificing important aspects of your life.

Your ability and willingness to view time as a priority and not a resource, and to reallocate it to your most important personal and professional needs will provide the immediate ability to better create and sustain meaning.

Keep a journal of two weeks of your activities. Record what you were doing and how much time you spent (e.g., meetings from 9 to 10:30, work on the Simpson Project 10:30 to noon, lunch to 1:15, and so forth). Include your work and home time. Then add it up after the two weeks and you may just be surprised that the great preponderance of your time is being spent on very low-impact issues with little or no return.[*]

You need time to create meaning. No one's legacy has ever been, "They were important contributors in meetings and were always on time and never left early."

True Spirituality

Let's define "spirituality" in this manner: the quality of being concerned with the human spirit or soul as opposed to material or physical things. I'm not talking about religion, though people of faith may well be spiritual.

---

[*] Which always raises the questions, should I try to fix the lawn mower or call a repair shop? Should I wash the car or run it though the car wash?

I'm talking about our connection with the world around us. We need to stop worrying about people catching up and passing us and begin looking around in appreciation of who we are and where we are.

I used the example of the robins and the worms earlier. I first thought about this watching the robins hop around the lawn and sit on the fence railings. After taking the time to watch them for several minutes, I saw some pulling worms from the grass. That's when I began thinking about the "early bird" success, but also realized that worm would not have a good day.

I read recently about a beetle that is food for some frogs, as are many insects. But this particular beetle has the capacity to crawl through the frog's digestive system in six minutes, causing it to defecate, and the beetle is thrust out perfectly fine though somewhat soiled. The frog's digestive system would normally take over a day to process food.

That caused me to wonder about how people adapt to seemingly dire situations. When a prospect is cynical because I don't have staff, or am from the east coast, or have never worked in his or her industry, I reply, "That's exactly why you need me!" I turn the tables and ask if they'd like to have some fresh air or continue breathing their own exhaust. I refuse to be "digested."*

You're safest in the eye of the storm. If you're in a rip tide, you don't swim against it you swim perpendicular to it (parallel to the shore). Many retailers in tough times raised the prices of their products and experienced a resurgence of business and profit, doing nothing else at all. People assumed they were getting what they paid for and the higher price denoted, to them, higher value.

There's our beetle example.

My point is that we have to take the time to look around if we are to create meaning. You don't appreciate neighborhoods flying over them in a plane at 35,000 feet. And you don't ever appreciate the plane if you simply bury your head in a book, or watch a movie, or sleep. I've watched how the cabin crew works on long flights, and marveled at how flight attendants I

---

* Though I'm not talking about religion, it does remind me of the story of Jonah and the whale!

hadn't met still called me by my name. I wondered why hotels and restaurants couldn't always manage that.

I read an article recently about a professional woman who purchased a motorcycle she had always wanted, had it restored, and drove it every weekend. She said that she always took freeways in her car, always the fastest route. But on the bike she wanted the slowest route, the back roads, because she wanted to see all that she could and experience the benefits of the bike. I thought that was great insight.

We need to appreciate our place on earth, our relationships within our families, our relationships with others, and our relationships with our environment. I've been stunned when I've taken a commuter train, which I rarely do, and found that there was a culture involved: who took which seats, where coats were placed, how to drink coffee and eat a bun, even how to board and disembark; I found myself scorned for breaking the rules I didn't understand.

Those rules didn't help the commute. They simply placed people in a routine so as not to have to be "present." And as I looked around trying to appreciate this environment, I saw people who arose in the morning, commuted to work, performed their jobs, commuted home, had dinner, watched TV, and went to bed—all a constant routine with no true understanding or insight into their daily rituals. They were doing this without thinking, without understanding.

Here's a hint: When your seat is always saved for you, and the server says "the usual?," and you're upset when the train or bus is not as it "should be," it's time to make some changes.

Spirituality is about understanding the people and the world around us. But to do that, we need both the time and intent. We need to appreciate the worm, not just the bird, the beetle, not merely the frog, the back roads, not solely the highways. We need to stop seeing ourselves as the center of the universe but merely as a small part of it. Our "human xenophobia" can be stifling.

A mayfly lives for one day. Certain cicadas surface only once every 17 years. There is a kind of clam known as a "quahog" that has been found at 500 years old, and going strong. The coelacanth fish was thought to be extinct at the end of the Cretaceous Period *about 140 million years ago*, but was discovered alive and well in the 1930s, virtually unchanged from fossil evidence. They've recently found a dwarf kind of elephant in the horn of Africa that scientists had thought extinct for nearly a century. No one told the elephants.

And I'll remind you that scientists believe modern humans to be about 200,000 years old. The dinosaurs lived for 120 million years, and only died out after a huge piece of space junk hit the Yucatan.

Spirituality requires some perspective.

CHAPTER 10

How Green Can Grass Get?

The grass may be greener, but so the hell what? How green can green be? That's in the eye of the beholder. Happiness has to be on our own terms, not from some celebrity, or glossy magazine, or braggart neighbor. You have to be comfortable sailing through life in the manner that pleases you. It's not about the size of the craft, because there is always going to be a bigger boat. Stop trying to buy and build bigger boats. Start looking for happy sailing.

The Reciprocity of Happiness

We were at the harbor in St. Bart's in the Caribbean. The slips were filled with multi-million-dollar yachts. Standing by themselves, they may have been impressive. But docked together with no elbow room and no perspective to see the entire boat, they looked like large cars crammed into a parking lot on a busy shopping day. Farther out in the harbor, barely detailed from shore, were the even larger yachts that couldn't fit in the slips. For all of their size and majesty, they couldn't be seen or appreciated.

I know some of you are thinking, "That's okay, they please the owners in and of themselves." Well, if that's the case, why the obsession with the biggest boat, the fastest car, the most glittery gem? These baubles, large and small, are meant to be seen. They are public extensions of the owners, no less than clothing, makeup, or a hairdo.

This isn't restricted to tangible items or movement. There are obsessions with perfect lawns, where every blade of grass is inspected and groomed, chemically treated, and hydrologically sated. There are lawns like carpets or even better than carpets. I met a woman who showed me photos of her fruits and vegetables, explaining her all-natural approach, and the need to buy $500 of chicken manure.

"You purchased $500 dollars of chicken poop?" I asked, incredulously.

How green can grass get? How big can a squash grow? Do you name them, and is cooking them akin to cannibalism or devouring a family member? I'm just sayin'…

I don't think we have the right to consume happiness without also creating it. Happiness is reciprocal. It's been said that all humor is based on someone's pain, from a pratfall to a political observation. But that's not true of happiness. Just standing on a beach looking at the ocean, or watching your children, or playing with the dog—these can be acts of sheer happiness.

But the question becomes, what are we contributing? Is our happiness at the expense of others, creating that humor that originates in others' pain? Is our happiness present because we denied someone else, we refused to sacrifice to pursue selfish ends? Is our happiness due to cheating?

Case Study: The Sales Philosophy Scammer

I wrote back to one of these scammers once who was promising to provide an inheritance if I'd first send money, asking how he could so blatantly try to cheat people. You know the story. He actually wrote back, trying to get me to "invest." Again, I asked how he could engage in such illegal and unethical acts.

Astoundingly, he quoted passages from Zig Zigler, Dale Carnegie, Tony Robbins, Napoleon Hill, and Og Mandino! He was applying these "motivational methods" to his own, illicit work. He believed he was working hard and remaining positive—in pursuing illegal activity and cheating people!

Peter Drucker famously observed that the goal of a company is to have a customer. I would simply add "a happy, profitable customer." When you create happy customers they return the favor with their business and referrals. You've created *meaning* in such transactions. When people are loyal they will always provide us with the benefit of the doubt. When Emirates Airlines is late, most passengers believe it was unavoidable. When United Airlines is late, most passengers think of conspiracies.

There is always a bigger boat, there is always greener grass. We deserve happiness, we should pursue happiness, not simply bigger toys. But the most meaningful way to create it for ourselves is to generate it for others. If you run through that open gate, and then look back at your own yard, you might just find the grass is greener there.

We invest a great deal of our energy in avoiding meaning. Our focus tends to default to acquisition, safeguarding former acquisitions, not losing ground to others who may be gaining, trying to impress others. I heard a palliative care nurse say once that most people who express regrets at the end of their lives are referring to things they failed to do.

The Psychic Investment Has a Poor ROI

We are so overcome with obtaining and achieving and succeeding that we become oblivious to our actual existence. Disneyland provides entertainment with façades. There is piping, and mechanisms, and employee

passageways behind and underneath the attractions, and actors in the cos-
tumes. It's been said that modern Venice is a façade, with lovely hotels and
buildings facing the canals for tourists but no local population remaining.
If you tour Venice with a private guide you find buildings boarded up, used
by foreigners a few times a year, playgrounds empty, and local shops out of
business.

It has become a Disneyland for adults.

What are we investing our time in, and what is the return? I tend to keel
over laughing when I encounter people on social media or sending me email
with 20 initials after their names: Joan Smith, MBA, PC-F, CCA, CMFA,
PE, RspNF, and on and on and on.* At conferences, which provide ribbons
for name tags based on accomplishments, you'll see people with dozens of
ribbons flowing toward their waists, like medals on a rear admiral. These
attempts to impress through appearance occur in dozens of ways, including uniforms and accessories. (The wit Dorothy Parker, leaving dinner at a
hotel, was said to have asked the doorman for a cab. "Madam," he said, "I'm
no doorman, I'm a vice admiral in the Navy!" "Great," she replied, "then
get me a destroyer.")

People become quite irritated when I remark on the initial excess,
explaining that the strings of initials are recognized in their professions,
they earned them all, they add credibility, yada yada yada. They are, in
fact, an attempt to create gravitas, respect, and status not with behavior and
expertise, but with the same kind of façade used at Disneyland and Venice.

This becomes such an intense competition that people started to put
MA after their names, standing for "master of arts," which no one ever does
who's not desperate for recognition and status. For a while I assumed they
were all from Massachusetts.

The quest for "bigger" or "faster" or even "smaller" (as in smart phones
or computers) obscures the meaning we need to create in our lives. I'm
convinced that one's mindset—that pessimism or optimism—controls

---

* I was amazed when I found I could string 19 initials after my own name. These things drop like
confetti from trade and professional organizations.

one's day. In the morning, some people arise and believe it's another day of opportunity and delight and the potential to create and enjoy happiness. Others get out of bed and think that it's another long day of a slow crawl through enemy territory.

Have you ever encountered someone at their job who's already nasty at opening time, in a restaurant, or at a ticket counter, or a security desk, or a train? We all have. What's the rest of their day going to be like? I assure you, in most cases it's not an odd occurrence but their usual state of mind no matter at what stage of the day.

I talked earlier of time being a priority, not a resource. I'm suggesting here that we reallocate our time to a greater return from merely acquiring and collecting and seeking status. We should allocate it to achieving happiness by creating happiness and by creating meaning for ourselves. I want to emphasize "for ourselves." I'm in the Speakers Hall of Fame® and I'm weary of "motivational" speakers who chain-smoke, or are morbidly obese, or who are on their third marriage, telling the audience to "take control of your lives"! They are certainly not the ones to create meaning for us. (My father used to tell me, when I found his rules hypocritical, "Do as I say, not as I do!" I found that to be 100 percent ineffective in terms of influencing my behavior.)

We need to work against our own metrics, not those of others. My happiness, my meaning, needn't be yours and yours needn't be mine; hence, I eschew the "search" for meaning. The search for tangible proof of one's worth, the constant competition to maintain that status, and the race to perform better and be happier by others' standards are all the wrong metrics.

They constitute a terrible psychic return on that investment.

Being Green

Jim Henson's Muppets have been a brilliant entertainment and educational institution and, for me, I've recognized Kermit the Frog as their ringleader, or emcee, or charismatic center. His canonical rendition of "It Ain't Easy

Being Green" is a paean to being different in a world trying to make us all the same, homogenized, and/or making us outcasts and lower status if we're different. I'm suggesting that there is an advantage to being the exception, to being different, to being green.

Just as we imperfectly strive to accept and include diversity in ethnicity, origins, gender, lifestyles, physical ability, talents, and so forth, we should strive to welcome the diversity in ourselves. Attempts to meet other people's standards, others' demands, others' expectations are futile. We've seen gifted kids receive poor marks and even behavioral criticism in school because they were actually bored and were trying to fulfill themselves.

We're amazed when an athlete succeeds with a different grip, a different approach, a different technique. The "Fosbury Flop" radically changed high jumping and enabled new records (without better equipment or illegal drugs, merely a change in body position). Soccer-style kicking changed the game in American football. As I write this, Jerry James, a former body builder and wrestler, is hitting such long drives in golf that the hide-bound sporting authorities are concerned about the implications.

Sandy Koufax of the Dodgers, for my money the greatest pitcher in history, studied the mechanics of the body when pitching to learn now best to throw hard and accurately.* The saxophonist Kenny G can hold one note for 40 minutes because he learned to breathe in through his nose and out through his mouth simultaneously.

Fred Smith decided that FedEx would deliver packages by using a hub in Memphis and not sending door-to-door, nonstop. Uber decided that taxi service could be clean, on call, and utilize GPS. Airbnb realized that travelers might prefer private, intimate lodging over mammoth, impersonal hotels. Streaming has closed movie theaters.

And on it goes, in every field.

Rejoice in being willing to be different, which is a precondition to actually being different. Airbnb has a different meaning from Marriott. FedEx is

---

* One year he was 27-5 with a Dodger team averaging less than two runs a game, and his lifetime World Series earned run average is .67.

different from the postal service. Sinatra didn't sing songs like everyone else. He told stories of love and loss and loneliness.

Grass can't get any greener when it's healthy. There is a finality to its greenness. But we can create more and more meaning, not trying to "outdo" others but merely by trying continually to satisfy ourselves in our contributions and behaviors. We need to stop creating more stuff and bigger things, and spend more time creating meaning.

Our legacy will not be about how green our grass was, metaphorically or literally.

Jerry Seinfeld, delivering a eulogy on his comedy show, once said that surveys showed that people were more afraid of public speaking than of dying. "In other words," he said, gesturing toward the casket, "I should be in worse shape than he is."

We do go through life fearfully because we shield ourselves from reality through ritual and routine, rote and regimen. We don't seek diversity or heterogeneity, we seek similarity and sameness. And we don't create meaning, we adopt other peoples' meaning, society's meaning, "normative meaning." We don't create our own. We're concerned about the size of our boat, or the initials after our names, or the ribbons on our chests. We're concerned about how we look to others, compared to others, judged by others.

Even if the result is something so big that it can't fit into the slips and can barely be seen from shore. Don't misunderstand, I don't mind people gaining wealth and having possessions, but I find that stupefyingly shallow if that's what the story of their life is about.

There's something wrong when the eulogy is about the size of the boat or the condition of the lawn. In fact, there's something wrong when the daily consideration of people is about such transient issues.

I've revised the chart from the introduction here in Figure 10.1. I hope you can now see your way to mastery. We've come to the end of the book and the beginning of your new approach to creating meaning. I realize I've provided philosophical as well as specific ideas, and I think you deserve my clear techniques for contributing to your ongoing legacy through the creation of meaning.

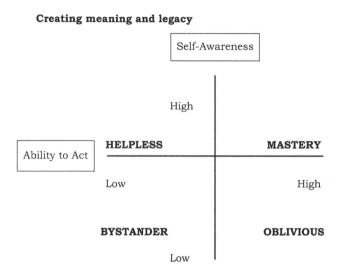

Figure 10.1 *Meaning and legacy.*

Creating Meaning and Legacy

So, to instantiate the key elements of creating meaning consider the steps below. And remember the chart from the introduction, included above. You don't want to be a bystander to your own life.

- We have no right to consume happiness and wealth without also creating happiness and wealth. *Contribute to the world around you.*
- Meaning is intensely personal. *Don't use other people's metrics for meaning, create your own.*
- Legacy is daily. *This isn't something to put off or procrastinate about. What can you do today to create meaning?*
- Your "book of life" turns a page every day, no matter what. *What can you add to your life, and those of others, daily, to make sure you're writing the book and no one else is, or that each page isn't blank?*
- Competition can become an addiction that you're not even aware of. *Stop trying to outdo everyone, simply be the best you can be, aware of your talents and skills and their applicability.*

- There is always a bigger boat. *You'll never have the largest or best or fastest, so learn to be happy with what's pleasing to you, personally, regardless of what others pursue.*
- There are no "overdogs" or "underdogs." *You create the heaviest, best shooting battalions by being different and true to yourself. Fight for what you believe in, don't be a part of the mob.*
- A hundredth of an inch or a second is ridiculous. *You can succeed without "winning," and winning is often arbitrary and subjective. Set your own goals and change them as you see fit.*
- Vulnerability is the key to intimacy. *Find people who will be honest with you and then allow them to be honest with you. Provide the same service to them.*
- Success, not perfection. *Don't strive for perfection, which kills excellence and leads to procrastination. Strive for success not perfection, chase happiness, not money.*
- It's easy to fake success, but why bother? *Finish the race in 20th place by training hard and focusing, not by taking the subway and pretending. Be honest enough to allow others to appreciate your true efforts.*
- Be comfortable being spiritual. *Observe and embrace the world around you. Use your learning "in the moment" to contribute to your meaning. What can you learn daily from what you hear, see, smell, touch, and experience?*
- The grass isn't always greener, nor does it matter. *Run through the open gate to find new experiences and ideas, and stop searching for some elusive meaning so that you can create your own. It's fine for you to be "green," though it ain't easy, in terms of being your own person with your own values and a unique legacy.*

The people around the world who have read my books, attended my speeches, participated in my coaching, and engaged with my online Forums are my legacy, growing and expanding every day. I see the future and light and promise through them in a myriad of countries, at a variety of ages, with a diversity of insights.

I wish you the same journey, the same ability to achieve meaning and see your legacy unfold in others and in your own growth. The reciprocity of helping others to grow, thereby growing yourself, and therefore being able to help others grow still more is powerful.

It brings meaning to my life and a legacy to my days.

Appendix

Resources: there are free newsletters, audio, video, and other materials on my website: https://alanweiss.com.

You can also enjoy my weekly podcast, *The Uncomfortable Truth*, and monthly video, The Writing on the Wall, on my blog on that site. You can also follow me on Twitter (http://twitter.com/BentleyGTCSpeed) and LinkedIn.

If you would like to take a free Legacy evaluation, with feedback about your current state as compared to others, you may do so by accessing this link:

AlanWeiss.com/LegacyAppendix

Index

Printed in the United States
by Baker & Taylor Publisher Services